Shazia Rahman

hotels • palaces • havelis • spas

indiachic

if your loyalty card is missing, please visit www.theworldsbesthotels.com

hotels · palaces · havelis · spas

indiachic

text inderjit badhwar · susan leong

BOLDING BOOKS

publisher'sacknowledgements

Welcome to *India Chic*—a magical journey through the very best of India at a time when the country has never been in better shape to welcome travellers looking for luxury, tranquillity, excitement, great food and wonderful people. You will find some fabulous properties featured within these pages and a million reasons to visit India now. Not only are more world-class properties opening their doors here, but the country is being increasingly well served by airlines from Europe and Asia, making the number of available flights and fares better still!

I must thank those who have made *India Chic* possible: our partners at Abercrombie and Kent, whose suggested itineraries are in the book; Mary Anne Denison Pender of Mahout, who has an irresistible collection of very chic properties and an equally irresistible charm; Peter Leitgeb of Leela Hotels and his chairman Captain Krishnan Nair for their kindness and hospitality; Joerg and Txuku of Malabar House; Ingo Schweder of Mandarin Oriental Hotels; and to the many other hoteliers in India for their support. As always, I am indebted to the very professional team at Editions Didier Millet for putting this book together and to you, the reader, for buying it. I hope the book inspires you to visit India and to stay in some of these wonderful places.

Nigel Bolding
editor-in-chief

executive editor
melisa teo

editors
laura jeanne gobal • geetha menon

designers
annie teo • lisa damayanti

production manager
sin kam cheong

first published in 2006 by
bolding books
49 wodeland avenue,
guildford gu2 4jz, united kingdom
enquiries : nigel.bolding@theworldsbesthotels.com
website : www.theworldsbesthotels.com

designed and produced by
editions didier millet pte ltd
121 telok ayer street, #03-01
singapore 068590
telephone : +65 6324 9260
facsimile : +65 6324 9261
enquiries : edm@edmbooks.com.sg
website : www.edmbooks.com

©2006 bolding books
design and layout © editions didier millet pte ltd

Printed in Singapore

isbn: 981-4155-57-8

COVER CAPTIONS:

1, 2 + 9: *The regal Oberoi Udaivilās.*
3: *A boat on Lake Pichola.*
4: *Elephants dressed for a festival.*
5: *Panels at The Leela, Goa.*
6: *A close-up of a decorated elephant.*
7: *A temple in south India.*
8: *Indian cuisine.*
10: *A lavishly adorned Rajasthani lady.*
11: *Jantar Mantar in Jaipur.*
12: *Yoga at Wildflower Hall.*
13: *Textiles for sale in Goa.*
14: *An oil lamp at The Leela, Goa.*
15: *The courtyard at Rambagh Palace.*
16 + 19: *A room and dining facilities at Devi Garh Fort Palace.*
17: *Evening aarti at Rishikesh.*
18: *Hats for sale outside a mosque in Bangalore.*
20: *A carved exterior at Fatehpur Sikri.*
21–23: *The opulent Taj Lake Palace.*

PAGE 2: *A well-kept courtyard at The Oberoi Udaivilās.*

THIS PAGE AND OPPOSITE: *Clean and simple interiors at Devi Garh Fort Palace.*

PAGE 8 AND 9: *The stylish pool area at The Park, Chennai.*

contents

thehimalayas 24

eastindia 46

centralindia 62

indiabystates

indiabychapters

Iran

Arabian Sea

The Himalayas

Rajasthan

Central
India

The Himalayas

East India

East India

The Arabian Coast

South India

South India

East India

introduction

fantasy and reality

India is not a destination, it is an experience. Think about India and the adjectives fly fast and furious. Inscrutable India. Impossible India. Intriguing India. Phantom India, as French film-maker Louis Malle described it. Exasperating. Indiscernible. Undisciplined. Infinite. Unfortunately, since India as a subject is neglected in the curricula of most Western school systems, the perceptions come mostly from the media, which concentrates on headline-making news like wife-burning, caste violence, Hindu-Muslim religious riots and, of course, poverty.

In the 1950s and 1960s, American parents would exhort their children to wipe their dinner plates clean with the moral sermon that people in India and China were starving. Recalling this, Pulitzer Prize-winning *New York Times* columnist Thomas Friedman remarks on the attitudinal change that has occurred. In his recent best-seller, *The World Is Flat*, he writes, 'I now tell my daughters, "Finish your homework. People in India and China are starving for your job."' His allusion was to the fact that technology and market reform are flattening the world in which India and China are emerging as the early winners. Friedman also observed, 'Indeed, there is a huge famine breaking out all over India today, an incredible hunger, but it is not for food. It is a hunger for opportunity that has been pent up like volcanic lava under four decades of socialism, and it's now just bursting out with India's young generation.'

Chroniclers like Friedman are trailblazing a different kind of journalism—perhaps similar to that of the ancient Chinese travellers like Fah Yen-Yan (5th century) and Hun Yen-Sang (7th century)—in which they abjure sensationalism and instant analysis, penetrate the core of changes occurring within distant countries, and shatter preconceived notions. To explore just how explosive these changes are in today's India, you need to visit just one Indian city, Bangalore, the new Silicon Valley in south India, which is fast becoming the outsourcing capital of the world. But even though economic parameters are a useful guide to a nation's psyche, a nation's sense of its self emanates also from its underlying vibrancy, the captivating quality of seas and

THIS PAGE: India is a country full of colour, with a people who display an exuberance for life.
OPPOSITE: The Taj Mahal, the country's most famous landmark and a monument to love.

mountains, the institutional memory of the creativity and spiritual yearnings of its forbears. In these, India has been blessed with a bountiful harvest of riches.

lighting up the world

India's civilisation dates back to between 7000 BC and 5000 BC when the Harappans created cities of unparalleled dignity in the Indus Valley. However, this civilisation vanished mysteriously. The Aryans gave the world Sanskrit, metaphysics, astronomy and the beautiful verses of the Vedas, which date back to between 3000 BC and 2000 BC, from which also sprang the great religions of the world—Hinduism, Buddhism, Jainism, and later, Sikhism. But for centuries, the inheritors of this Vedic or Sanskrit civilisation were invaded by marauders, iconoclasts and

THIS PAGE: The Red Fort, a legacy of Mughal rule.

OPPOSITE (TOP): Jainism is a classical religion with its origins in the prehistory of India.

adventurers—the Huns, Scythians, Parthians and Greeks, and the hordes of Central Asia: the Turks, Afghans and Mongols, followed by the Portuguese, Dutch and British.

India was valued for its gold, pre-Christian temple architecture, epics, centres of learning, philosophy and scholarship. Universities like Nalanda, founded in the 5th century AD, and its great library, were destroyed. Temples were plundered, sculptures defaced, poets killed, and India's people converted at the point of the sword to different religions.

But India epitomises the resilience of the human spirit. This ancient race embraced even the invaders and survived to tell its story. Hindu and Muslim architecture combined to produce the grandiose Mughal architecture of the Taj Mahal and New Delhi's Red Fort. A new language combining Hindi and the language of the invading

Central Asians was born in the beautiful form of Urdu. The colonial architecture of Mumbai (previously Bombay), Kolkata (previously Calcutta) and New Delhi became part of the essential Indian landscape. And English came as a blessing in disguise, now giving India an advantage in the brave new world of globalisation.

The universalist transcendental philosophy of the Vedas and Upanishads has inspired writers such as Emerson, Whitman, Thoreau and H. G. Wells. Alexander Hamilton, upon his return from India in 1802, taught Sanskrit to Friedrich von Schlegel, the great German critic who spread the knowledge of this language in Germany. His brother, August, translated the Bhagavad Gita into Latin.

Raaga, the music born in Vedic India, is perhaps India's greatest artistic gift to the world. Sitarist Ravi Shankar, who took this musical form to the West, even won over the Beatles and classical violinist Yehudi Menuhin. French flautist Jean Pierre Ramphal considers Indian *raaga* flautist Hari Prasad Chaurasia one of the world's greatest artistic geniuses. Modern gurus like Oshō, Krishnamurti and Maharishi Mahesh Yogi popularised the complex philosophical idiom of Vedantic thought, and institutionalised its wisdom in *ashrams* across the world. The marvels of Indian rock-cut architecture, and temples and stupas dating back to thousands of years before the birth of Christ, continuing past the Middle Ages, draw millions of tourists to this subcontinent.

India is a country of more than a dozen officially recognised languages and 24 other major languages. There are also hundreds of dialects spoken, some of which resemble Swahili and Chinese. English has earned India recognition for literature and poetry. The names of authors of Indian origin—Ved Mehta, Salman Rushdie,

Vikram Seth, R. K. Narayanan, V. S. Naipaul, Anita Desai, Jhumpa Lahiri, Nirad C. Chowdhuri and Rabindranath Tagore, to name only a few—are legendary.

Indian cuisine also reflects the country's mixed heritage. Tandoori chicken, for example, originates from the Mughals who invaded India from Central Asia. The food of Goa is influenced by the Portuguese. And the original mutton cutlet, once the *pièce de résistance* of Britain's *haute cuisine*, is available in select Indian restaurants.

THIS PAGE (FROM LEFT): *Mahatma Gandhi's non-violent struggle for India's independence drew millions of supporters; a grand Republic Day parade.*

OPPOSITE (FROM TOP): *The ruins of Nalanda, one of the first universities in the world; the sitar is a classical Indian musical instrument.*

wheels of continuity

By the 19th century, Britain had assumed political control of virtually all Indian lands. Mahatma Gandhi and Jawaharlal Nehru (India's first prime minister) led the nationalist

struggle for independence in 1947. The subcontinent was divided into the secular state of India and the Muslim state of Pakistan. A third war between the two countries in 1971 resulted in east Pakistan becoming the separate nation of Bangladesh. India continues to function as the world's largest democracy, with regular general and state assembly elections, an independent judiciary, and a lively and unshackled press with independent television stations now playing a bigger role in investigative reporting. Until the late 1980s, Nehru's party, the Indian National Congress, ruled the nation with huge majorities. But with regional and ethnic forces becoming politically stronger, the nation has moved into an era of coalition politics.

In 2004, the country held its five-yearly general election in which more than 650 million people cast their votes to elect 552 of their chosen representatives for the Lower House (nationally known as Lok Sabha) of the country's Parliament. In the 14th Parliament that was formed as a result, the ruling Bharatiya Janata Party-led coalition was replaced by one led by Indian National Congress president Sonia Gandhi, wife of the late prime minister Rajiv Gandhi, Nehru's grandson.

from ocean to sky

Modern India is a constitutional republic consisting of 28 mostly autonomous states and six union territories administered by proxy from New Delhi. With over a billion inhabitants accounting for more than one-sixth of the world's total population, India is the second most populous country after China. The land mass of India, together with Bangladesh and most of Pakistan, forms a well-defined subcontinent set apart from the rest of Asia by the imposing northern mountain rampart of the Himalayas and by lesser adjoining mountain ranges to the west and east. In area, India ranks as the seventh-largest country in the world, covering 3,287,590 sq km (1,269,369 sq miles).

India's topographical and geographical diversity is mind-boggling. It is a land of vast deserts, sparkling seas, diverse wetlands, great mountain ranges, and villages, towns and cities of all sizes. The country's long coastline extends over 5,700 km (3,542 miles). There are three distinct physical regions: the mountainous Himalayan

THIS PAGE: Across the country's vast, changing landscape, a rich architectural heritage is visible.

OPPOSITE (FROM TOP): The Ganges is India's most sacred river; brightly hued trucks carry India's goods to the country's ports for export around the world.

zone in the north, reaching across to the northwest and northeast, the Indo-Gangetic plain and the Deccan peninsula, which is separated from the great river plains by the Vindhaya mountains.

India also has four clearly defined river systems covering the Himalayas, the Deccan plateau, and the coastal and inland drainage basins. The Himalayan rivers, being snow-fed, are perennial. The basin of the Ganges is the largest, draining about a quarter of the country. As famous Indian naturalist and film-maker Kunal Verma says, 'In India each river is considered to have a life of its own, its own presiding deity. It is not just an inanimate gush of water but suffused with divine energy, life giving and purifying.' He adds, 'For the *rishis* (India's ancient sages) the journey of a river from its source right across to the ocean was symbolic of human life going through all the myriads of worldly experiences to merge finally in the ocean.' Treating rivers as divine was not just superstition, but rather an effort to impress upon man that he had to live in nature in harmony with everything else, and not as a lord and master who exploited nature. Nature treated with reverence would provide amply, nature abused would inflict painful calamities.

It is no wonder the Ganges, the river of Lord Shiva, is revered as *mata* (mother) and the Yamuna is treated as Lord Krishna's river. The Indo-Gangetic Valley provided the country with the largest tract of rich agricultural land, becoming the country's most densely populated area and the cradle of Indian civilisation.

riding the future

Modern India is all around. A middle class estimated at nearly 300 million people with world-class purchasing power, and rural markets emerging as prime investment destinations for Indian companies and MNCs (multi-national corporations) prove that the country's economy is on the rise. Indian merchandise exports have doubled to US$80 billion in the last three years. Exports of software and IT-enabled services have almost tripled to US$17.2 billion. India's software BPO exports have penetrated

400 of the Fortune 500 (the 500 biggest US corporations), emerging as the global research and development hub for MNCs.

India has one of the world's youngest populations—almost 70 per cent below the age of 35 and almost 50 per cent below the age of 25. True, large numbers of Indians still live in slums or villages, but expectations are rising, as is the demand for upward mobility. The idea that poverty is fated is disappearing. India's impressive strides in higher education have been recognised the world over. But now there is a growing demand that English be taught in state schools—where 85 per cent of children go—beginning in the first, not fourth grade. These aspirations are coming from farmers, and India's dispossessed and indigent castes.

atithi devo bhava

Many first-time visitors to India take back negative impressions, not about the nation's living heritage that is mesmerising, but about crammed waiting areas at airports, long queues at customs, rude immigration officials, tourist hustlers, poor connectivity between

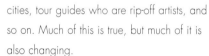

cities, tour guides who are rip-off artists, and so on. Much of this is true, but much of it is also changing.

India's Minister of State for Tourism, Renuka Chowdhury, is a dynamic young woman who has been able to convince the government that India's tourist industry has the potential to be the largest employment generator in the country, especially since tourism covers many sectors, from airlines to airports, ground transportation, hotels, shopkeepers and railroads. She is now implementing, with the help of other concerned ministries, a makeover of the entire infrastructure. Mumbai and New Delhi international airports, the main entry points, are being privatised and modernised to match the best in the world. Twenty-two new airports are being tendered for by private players in smaller destinations. New private airlines are being licensed. Shipping laws are being changed to allow cruise ships from Europe and other countries to ply Indian waters. Railway station waiting rooms are being air-conditioned and upgraded, and new budget hotels with prominently displayed rate cards are being encouraged through various concessions. Taxis are being equipped with monitoring devices and emergency alarm systems as a major crime-prevention device.

But the biggest initiative is *atithi devo bhava*. This Sanskrit adage, dear to all Indians, means 'a guest is like a god'. Under this mass education programme now entering its second phase, the ministry has trained thousands of people in the tourism industry—airport staff, porters, immigration officials, drivers, guides, hotel receptionists and shopkeepers—in areas such as basic English, courtesy, hygiene and honesty. After this training period, the participants receive ISO-type certificates approved by the ministry that they can display in their shops or vehicles, or ID cards. The certification is valid for a year, after which a refresher course is required.

unity in diversity

The vitality of the Indian tradition is based on socio-religious developments associated with ideas and practices connected with Vedic thought, Hinduism being one of its outcomes. Hinduism does not have a formal priesthood. Traditionally, the *sadhus* are people who have renounced the material pleasures of life. They, along with the semi-formal Brahmin clergymen, are looked upon as what can come closest to a priesthood. But Hinduism cannot excommunicate followers or pass *fatwas*, and does not believe in evangelism. You can be an atheist and you can still be a Hindu. You can marry outside your religion. You are not compelled to read the scriptures. And you

THIS PAGE (FROM TOP): *Decorative features epitomise the celebration of Indian festivals; many visitors to India leave with a new appreciation for their spirituality.*
OPPOSITE: *The 250-year-old Taj Lake Palace offers guests a glimpse of India's regal history.*

never even have to go to a temple. This is because Hinduism is all around, in architecture, philosophy, meditation, yoga, ethics, fairs, festivals, and in the celebration of socio-religious festivals like Holi and Diwali (also known as Deepavali) throughout the length and breadth of the land. It is a way and celebration of life.

The core Vedic philosophy as summed up in the Upanishads is that man's biggest mistake is not any 'original sin' but 'primordial ignorance' of his true place in the universe. This leads him to the mistaken notion that he lives outside of nature and the universe. And only when he realises—through the pursuit of truth, meditation and detachment—that his inner reality and what he perceives as the outside world are one holistic reality, will he be freed from the pain of everyday anxieties and suffering. In order to reach pure consciousness and joy, he must reposition himself. He must begin a journey of self-discovery, 'go within himself' and remove the veils (*maya*) that stand between him and enlightenment. Oxford lecturer and philosopher Juan Mascaro observes, 'Greece and India give us complementary views of the world. In the Greek temple we find the clear perfection of beauty, in the Indian temple we find the sublime sense of Infinity.'

The people of India are diverse, speaking in hundreds of tongues and dialects. In Kashmir, Indians are green-eyed and fair. In Punjab, they are Greek-looking. In the northeast they could pass for Chinese, Japanese, Korean or Vietnamese. In the Indo-Gangetic plains, they are dark-skinned with Caucasian features. In central India and parts of south India they could pass for Africans, Puerto Ricans or Mexicans. In Western Gujarat, they look Arabic or Semitic. Indians have strong regional and linguistic identities, and differing religious rituals, but they beautifully sum up the phrase 'unity in diversity'. Just take a look at the country's current key political movers: India's president, Abdul Kalam, is a Muslim, its prime minister, Manmohan Singh, is a Sikh, and the president of the party that heads the ruling coalition government, Sonia Gandhi, is an Italian-born Roman Catholic. To experience all of the subcontinent's diversity in one visit would be impossible.

It is a way and celebration of life.

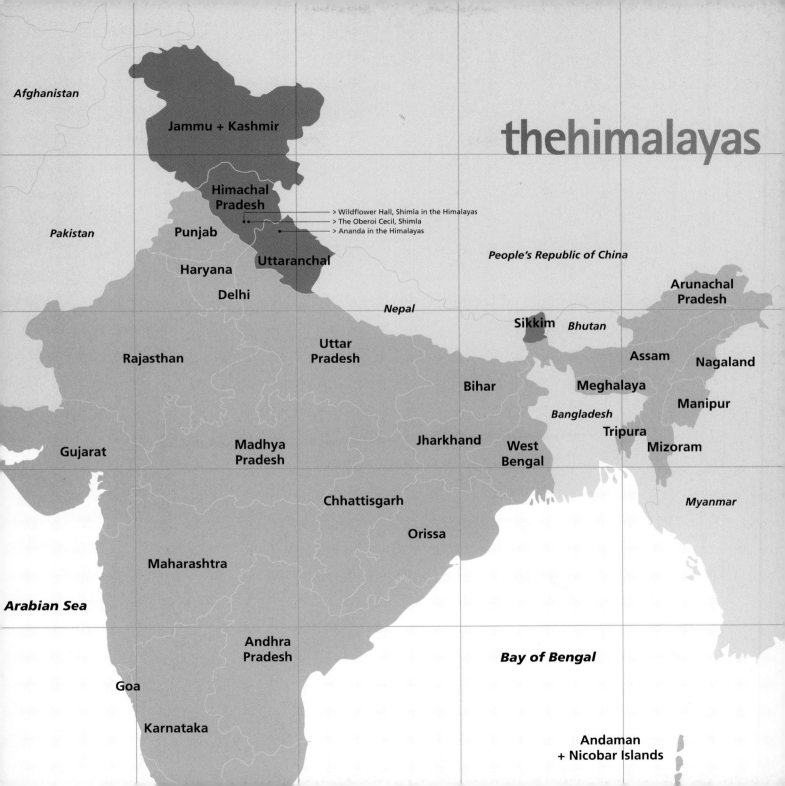

Afghanistan

Jammu + Kashmir

Himachal
Pradesh

> Wildflower Hall, Shimla in the Himalayas
> The Oberoi Cecil, Shimla
> Ananda in the Himalayas

Pakistan

Punjab

People's Republic of China

Haryana

Uttaranchal

Arunachal
Pradesh

Delhi

Nepal

Sikkim   Bhutan

Assam

Nagaland

Rajasthan

Uttar
Pradesh

Bihar

Meghalaya

Manipur

Gujarat

Madhya
Pradesh

Jharkhand

Bangladesh

Tripura

Mizoram

West
Bengal

Chhattisgarh

Myanmar

Orissa

Maharashtra

Arabian Sea

Andhra
Pradesh

Bay of Bengal

Goa

Karnataka

Andaman
+ Nicobar Islands

thehimalayas

the life-support system

The Himalayan range is a miraculous geological phenomenon. It is the world's highest natural fortress, dramatically separating the Indian subcontinent from the Tibetan Plateau. This belt of snow-clad mountains with the highest peaks in the world—Everest is more than 8,839 m (29,000 ft) high—traverses a course of 2,500 km (1,554 miles) between the Indus Valley in the northwest and the mighty Brahmaputra River in the east. The mountains protect northern India from the hostile climate of Central Asia. They form a wall off which India's monsoon currents—the moisture-laden winds that sustain life in the subcontinent—bounce back to irrigate the plains parched by blistering summers. Their glaciers, including the sacred Gangotri, fount of the Ganges, are the source of India's snow-fed rivers. Some 19 major rivers drain the Himalayan region before flowing into the plains. Of these, nine are a part of the Ganges and Yamuna systems, whose waters sustain life in the Indo-Gangetic plains.

Among these mountains, in the bliss of solitude, India's ancient sages meditated, found the wisdom that comes from the 'unknown' and shared their insights with disciples who spread across the land preaching the gospel of the eternal soul and the beauty of infinity. Within these rapturous surroundings, India's founding prime minister, Jawaharlal Nehru, wrote his masterful *The Discovery of India*. Adventurers like Sir Edmund Hillary and Tenzing Norgay scaled Everest. Other adventurers perished in avalanches or died of frostbite, hypothermia or pneumonia in sub-zero conditions.

PAGE 24: The mountains still attract adventurous souls.

THIS PAGE (FROM TOP): Shikaras ply the waters of Dal Lake; visit the birthplace of Ayurveda.

OPPOSITE: There is beauty even in stark surroundings.

the hills are alive

Yet the Himalayas are neither forbidding nor hostile. They are, in fact, effervescent with life, music, folk traditions, villages, sparkling mountain streams, lush vegetation, religious trails, Buddhist monasteries, Hindu temples, mountain resorts, hill stations, ski trails and even golf courses. This is because the Himalayas, despite their façade, are not homogenous. Their diversity is spectacular. The mountains cover regions that can be bleak and barren, or teeming with life and lush vegetation.

The Himalayas actually comprise three parallel ranges. The Sub-Himalayan range, known as the Siwalik hills in India, is the youngest of the three and rises to a height of 1,200 m (3,934 ft). The Lower Himalayan range, running parallel to this, has peaks between 2,000–5,000 m (6,562–16,404 ft) high and is home to many famous hill stations, including Shimla and Darjeeling. The final range is the Higher Himalayas, with peaks exceeding 6,000 m (19,685 ft). This is where Everest and K2 are found.

animal planet

Climates vary across the Himalayas and as a result, the region's flora and fauna are equally varied. Forests range from evergreen to sub-tropical, eastern temperate and alpine. The region's wildlife is just as diverse. In the terai regions of the Himalayan foothills roam elephants, gaurs (Indian wild buffalo), rhinoceros and a variety of antelopes. Animals in the cold desert of Ladakh include the red panda, yak, snow leopard and brown bear, to name a few.

stations beneath the peaks

Within the vast, cool expanse of the Lower Himalayan range, the British, during the era of the Raj, sought shelter from the scorching heat of the Indian plains where temperatures rise to 45° C (113° F) in the summer. Here, enjoying day-time temperatures of around 28° C (82° F) and night-time temperatures of between 5°–10° C (41°–50° F), they built great colonial towns in the form of hill stations. Parts of the Himalayas inspired homesickness among the British. They were reminded of Scottish hills and dales, the gently undulating English countryside, and even the Alps.

And so, they built their own little Scotlands and, for those who loved Europe, even their own Switzerlands in the Himalayas. Hill stations with exotic names like Shimla, Mussoorie, Dalhousie, Nainital and Ranikhet, were built in the hills, with material carted up to heights of 2,438 m (8,000 ft) on the backs of mules along dirt roads which were later converted into some of the finest mountain highways. The towns featured Scottish manors, Tudor and Elizabethan cottages, and Georgian refinement, with main roads lined with shops and eateries, and hotels with names like Savoy and Chapslee. Their dance floors were made of the finest pinewood and parquet; the bands played—and still play—swing, jazz and waltzes to which British ladies twirled and pirouetted with their British or aristocratic Indian partners while the Himalayan mists rolled in gently through French windows; and muffins, tea, meringues, roast lamb and poached eggs were served to guests by liveried waiters. Here, too, Christian missionaries, Protestant and Catholic, built schools with names like St Edmunds, Waverly Convent, St Thomas and Woodstock.

These hill stations still stand. Tourists flock here in their hundreds of thousands every year to experience the British legacy and be a part of the 'native' surroundings and folklore without which these towns could not have been conceived. The foundation for these hill stations was either an ancient village or a princely state.

THIS PAGE: Yaks and sheep graze in the eastern Himalayas.

OPPOSITE (FROM TOP): The region offers contrasting images of snow-capped peaks against lush green valleys; a villager in Ladakh dresses warmly for winter.

hello shimla

Shimla, in Himachal Pradesh, became the alpine summer capital of India. Here Gothic palaces were erected for viceroys, their families and servants by labourers scaling steep slopes with boulders weighing 30 kg (66 lb) on their backs. Shimla appears to skim a 12-km-long (7.5-mile-long), crescent-shaped ridge dotted with markets, libraries and promenades flanked by steep hillsides.

Shimla's climate demands light woollens in mid-summer. Here, you shiver at sundown when the mercury dips to 15° C (59° F). The unparalleled panorama of the Himalayan peaks that resemble snowmen wearing wizard-like hats will remain indelibly etched in the memory even after just one visit. Those who enjoy long walks may wander through forests of oak and blooming rhododendron. There are enchanting hotels right in Shimla, including Wildflower Hall and The Oberoi Cecil. A must-try is golf at Naldehra. This scenic, nine-hole course, located about 2,438 m (8,000 ft) up in the hills, and 23 km (14 miles) from Shimla, is surrounded by a fine boutique resort with Finnish-style cottages made from imported wood. The venue was originally laid out by the viceroy, Lord Curzon, at the end of the 19th century. So enamoured was he by the beauty of the location that he named his youngest daughter Alexandra Naldehra.

One of the most enchanting ways to travel to Shimla is on the 'toy train' that starts its journey in the foothills of Kalka and slowly winds its way upwards for 90 km (56 miles) along a tortuous mountain trail to Shimla in four hours.

One of the Raj's greatest legacies is Lawrence School, in nearby Sanawar, built for the children of British soldiers serving in India. It started as a military school but is today one of India's premier public schools, showcasing resplendent stone

THIS PAGE (FROM TOP): Shimla's colonial heritage is reflected in the architecture of Viceregal Lodge; the 'toy train' to Shimla offers a novel way to travel.
OPPOSITE: Winding roads lead to exciting adventures.

architecture, a chapel and a graveyard where the names of soldiers who died during the wars are displayed. In fact, the surrounding valleys, like Subatoo, a Gurkha regimental centre, are peppered with graveyards with great memorial stones on which are inscribed the names of Britain's soldiers, businessmen, officials, housewives and children, who succumbed to wars, the plague, cholera, dysentery, malaria and typhoid in the 18th and 19th centuries.

voyages of discovery

Himachal Pradesh, however, is more than just Shimla and its surroundings. It is a massive area traversing 55,673 sq km (21,496 sq miles), with changing climates, topography, and a diverse mix of people. The colours of the valleys of Kullu, Kinnaur and Kangra are fit for an artist's palette. And in contrast to this rainbow of hues stand the barren terrains of Lahaul and Spiti—forbidding, challenging and defying.

Himachal's never-let-you-down tourist circuits are sculpted along the state's rivers and mountains. You will find a plethora of tourist pamphlets and websites guiding you to different destinations. But it is best to follow the tried and tested routes, which still offer ample scope for fun and eco-adventures. The Himachal Tourist Department has singled out a number of voyages worth checking out. Snaking through the ravines, the unforgiving Sutlej River has been known to break every dam and man-made obstacle in its path. The Sutlej River Voyage takes you through the Siwalik foothills, filled with apple orchards, conifers and oak trees, while further uphill are ski slopes that encourage adventure. Tented tourism beckons during the season, usually October to May. These are not your typical tents, however. They are deluxe tents that come equipped with modern amenities, including luxurious bathrooms. Barbecues and evening

bonfires are still a feature though. The Beas Voyage, named after a gentler river, brings you through valleys with flower-bedecked meadows, and fields of apple trees, paddy patches and tidy rows of cornfields. As the local saying goes, 'The Sutlej rages, but the Beas sparkles.'

If you would like to visit Dharamsala, home of the Dalai Lama, embark on the Dhauladhar Voyage, named after the perennially snow-clad Dhauladhar mountains. This range overlooks the fabled Kangra Valley—one of the cradles of Himalayan folk music—where shepherds roam with their freely feeding herds, temple bells chime incessantly and tea plantations extend down gentle slopes.

Himachal's Tribal Voyage Circuit passes through a spectacular terrain of river valleys, cold desert mountains, high passes, snow-capped peaks, icy lakes and mighty glaciers—an exotic land dotted with monasteries. Skiing and ice skating buffs should travel to Solang Nalla (Manali), Narkanda and Rohtang Pass from January to March.

Heli-skiing facilities are available in Manali. River rafting down the Sutlej, Beas and Chenab rivers is a must for thrill-seekers. You can also try your hand at paragliding and hang-gliding in Bir, Manali, Bilaspur and Rohru, or trout-fishing in Sangla, Katrain and Barot.

mussoorie or bust

The other quaint hill station, Mussoorie, is in the newly-formed Indian state of Uttaranchal. It has gradually developed as a centre for education and business. Tourists, both domestic and foreign, make a beeline for its modern bungalows, restaurants that serve Indian and European cuisine, malls and sculpted botanical gardens with rides for children, home-made ice cream, spiced roasted peanuts and chick peas, and mountains of cotton candy. You can reach Mussoorie from Delhi within six hours by road or rail for a splendid weekend. The town offers superb views of peaks in the western Garhwal hills, including Banderpunch, that soars to 6,316 m (20,721 ft) and Swargarohini, at 6,252 m (20,512 ft).

Some 8 km (5 miles) from Mussoorie lies the cosy resort of Clouds End, named thus because, as local folklore has it, the clouds end here. Guests can plan their meals a day ahead, ordering whatever they would like before going to bed each night. Because Clouds End appears to be located at the end of the horizon and offers stunning views, it is popular with honeymooners and tourists.

Major Hindu pilgrimage sites like Kedarnath, Badrinath, Gangotri, Yamunotri, Haridwar and Rishikesh are not far from here. Must-visit places are Dehradun, 29 km (18 miles) away, Uttaranchal's bustling capital and seat of the Indian Military Academy and the Indian Forest Research Institute; and Rishikesh, known as Tapo Bhumi, or 'the place for meditation of the Gods'. Rishikesh is a sacred Hindu pilgrimage site because the Ganges prepares for its long journey into the plains here. Visitors will also appreciate it for river rafting, meditation with gurus who dwell in caves, rock-climbing and five-star tented tourism.

saying it with flowers

Uttaranchal is indeed a paradise for tourists with varied interests. Its national parks beckon animal lovers, adventure seekers and tourists from all over the world. The Corbett National Park—named after the hunter-naturalist and author of the best-seller *Man Eaters of Kumaon*, about 300 km (186 miles) from New Delhi, is spread over 525 sq km (203 sq miles). It is the most popular safari park in the Himalayan foothills. Various lodges and resorts are located within easy reach of the park. Visitors can travel by jeep or on an elephant's back with expert guides to spot wildlife, including tigers, deer, leopards, sloths, monkeys, crocodiles and wild boars, while golden orioles, parakeets, mynahs, bulbuls and thrushes sing from the branches of trees in one of India's most dense forests.

Tours to the alpine forests of Uttaranchal include treks to the Valley of Flowers with its profusion of anemones, asters, fritillarias, gentians, geraniums, larkspurs, lilies, orchids, poppies (including the Himalayan blue poppy), potentillas, primulas and marsh marigolds. UNESCO has declared the Valley of Flowers a World Heritage Site.

a paradise never lost

Way up north, beyond the Peer Panjal ranges in the paradise of Jammu and Kashmir, visitors can experience sizzling summers, rustling autumns, spectral springs and crisp winters, while strawberries, peaches, walnuts, apricots and apples take turns filling the baskets of vendors as the seasons change. In the capital Srinagar, 1,730 m (5,676 ft) above sea level, *shikara* (traditional boats) ply the waters of the Dal, Nagin and Anchar lakes, and the Jhelum River which flows through the town, giving it a striking resemblance to Venice. The golf course here is now part of the Asian PGA circuit. The newest accommodation option, with splendid bars and restaurants, and boat rides virtually at your doorstep, is the InterContinental, The Grand Palace, formerly the abode of the maharaja. The Mughal gardens, the unique Hazratbal mosque, and the hilltop Shankaracharya temple built in 2500 BC, are also worth visits.

THIS PAGE: **The Valley of Flowers in full bloom.**
OPPOSITE: **The Beas River glistens in the sunlight.**

ski and shop

Nearby Gulmarg, 2,730 m (8,957 ft) high, is an alpine meadow flanked by ski slopes. It has one of the world's highest golf courses, where tourists now crowd the greens in open defiance of militant threats. Shopping here will leave one with soft pashminas, papier-mâché artefacts, handwoven carpets and walnut candle stands, among other things. Foodies should definitely try the delicious *gushtaba* (meatballs in a fiery gravy) and *yakni* (chicken stew), topped off with *kava* (tea flavoured with saffron). Enthusiasts can spend a lifetime, if they wish, among the many monasteries of Ladakh, the state's high altitude desert.

darjeeling on my mind

Moving along the Himalayas to the northwest, we encounter the town which tea made, Darjeeling. This scenic hillside town is located about 650 km (404 miles) from Kolkata. The Tibetan Buddhist monastery, Ghoom, is the town's iconic landmark and houses a 4.6-m-high (15-ft-high) Maitreya Buddha. Also here is the Padmaja Naidu Himalayan Zoological Park. This is where visitors with kids should head to, to see Mowgli's Baloo (from *The Jungle Book* by Rudyard Kipling and the Disney movie of the same name)—the Himalayan black bear, snow leopards and other exotic wildlife. From Observatory Hill, visitors will find themselves mesmerised by breathtaking views of the entire Kanchenjunga range.

When visibility is good and the weather not too hostile (April to May and October to November), try the Darjeeling–Sandakphu–Phalut trek. According to state sources, trekking on this route is not too much of a hassle as trekkers do not require much luggage. The Gorkha Hill Council has provided huts and other facilities along the way, but it is advisable to carry your own sleeping bags. The arduous journey passes through low areas and extremely high ridges, which means the temperature varies quite a bit. Water is a necessity, especially during the longer stretches of the trek when it is not easily available. Meals are provided on the trek.

Another site that must be explored is the Bhutia Busty Gompa (*gompa* refers to a monastery). Though the Himalayan region has a large number of monasteries in stunning locations, this one in particular is unique because it stands like a masthead in front of the mighty Kanchenjunga range. The monastery's library holds a copy of the Tibetan Book of the Dead. It also has a tourist hotspot right next to it in the form of Chowrasta—a great shopping area for trinkets and tasty treats like *mo-mos* (dumplings).

Darjeeling's renowned Himalayan Mountaineering Institute runs training courses for mountaineers. It also has an excellent collection of mountaineering equipment that was used in various historical expeditions. All records of attempts made to conquer Mount Everest are carefully stored in the Mount Everest Museum. A powerful Veb Carl Zeiss Jena telescope capable of astronomical observations is installed at this institute and is of great interest to visitors. It was presented by Adolf Hitler to Maharaja Judh Shumsher Jung Bhabur Rana, Commander-in-Chief of the Royal Nepal Army, and was later inherited by his son General Shamsher Jung Bahadur Rana, who presented it to the Himalayan Mountaineering Institute in July 1961. You can view the Kanchenjunga range in intimate detail with this telescope.

THIS PAGE: *Pick up a packet of tea direct from the source.*

OPPOSITE: *The region is a haven for sports enthusiasts, offering everything from skiing to trekking and horseback riding.*

No visit to Darjeeling would be complete without a visit to its famous tea gardens. Tea was first planted here over 150 years ago by Dr A. Campbell, a British surgeon sent to the region as its superintendent. Today, along with tourism, tea cultivation is one of Darjeeling's biggest earners. Among the oldest plantations here is Happy Valley Tea Garden, where visitors can learn about tea picking, manufacturing and processing.

While in Darjeeling, buy your tickets in advance to ride the great ropeway—the first in India—that connects North Point at 2,134 m (7,000 ft) with Singla Bazaar, further down at 244 m (800 ft). The entire journey takes about 40 minutes to cover 8 km (5 miles) and promises stunning views.

of mists and mountains

Nobody has summed up the Himalayan experience better than India's greatest Sanskrit poet, Kalidasa. Over 1,500 years ago he wrote, 'In the north there is a mighty mountain by the name Himalaya—the abode of perpetual snow, fittingly called the Lord of Mountains, animated by Divinity as its soul and internal spirit. Spanning the wide land from the eastern to the western sea, he stands as it were, like the measuring rod of the Earth.'

This could be why so many have been drawn to this land of mountains, mists and abundant colour over the years. Various people speaking different languages have wandered into this region, either to escape religious and political persecution or to get away from the droughts and heat of the plains. They took their gods and goddesses, songs and dances with them, and settled amongst the deep gorges, lush green and golden valleys, flower-filled meadows, misty woods, icy rivers, awe-inspiring glaciers and enchanting lakes of the Himalayas. Then there are the many who arrive to conquer its mountains and explore the wilderness each year, taking back with them the experience of a lifetime, and crystal-clear memories of astounding beauty. But one lifetime, as the saying goes, is not enough to understand, experience and roam through even a minuscule part of this region.

THIS PAGE: *Prayer flags flutter in the wind in Darjeeling;*
OPPOSITE: *Darjeeling's quaint hillside location still draws many tourists.*

...so many have been drawn to this land of mountains, mists and abundant colour...

Ananda in the Himalayas

Wake up to a panoramic view of mountains and valleys. Inhale deeply and fill your lungs with crisp, clean air tinged with the scent of flowers and trees. Start the day right with a fresh salad and juice, and move at a languid pace in line with the new, relaxed you. At Ananda in the Himalayas, a beautiful retreat located at the foothills of the spectacular Himalayas, you can achieve an idyllic routine which others just dream of.

Set amidst some 40 hectares (100 acres) of unspoilt natural terrain, Ananda overlooks the sacred Ganges River and Rishikesh Valley, and is housed in the former palaces of a maharajah and viceroy. To complement the unparalleled majesty of the Himalayas, the buildings have been restored to their original glory, complete with Moorish, Italian Renaissance and Indian architecture.

The design of the interior is a reflection of the region's colonial era, with fireplaces in the sitting room, high ceilings finished with 19th-century stamped-and-pressed copper, and Venetian crystal chandeliers for illumination. The Maharaja's Library is a treasure trove, with shelves bearing more than 1,000 rare books on ancient medicinal sciences from the maharaja's personal

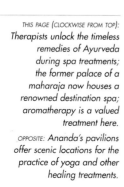

THIS PAGE (CLOCKWISE FROM TOP): Therapists unlock the timeless remedies of Ayurveda during spa treatments; the former palace of a maharaja now houses a renowned destination spa; aromatherapy is a valued treatment here.
OPPOSITE: Ananda's pavilions offer scenic locations for the practice of yoga and other healing treatments.

collection. Even his 150-year-old hand-carved billiard table and personal cues are available for use.

Ananda aims to rejuvenate the body, mind and soul of every person who steps through its door, and the location of the property—at the birthplace of India's ancient arts of yoga, meditation and Ayurveda—is the inspirational wellspring of the spa's treatments and therapies.

Ananda is a true destination spa, where everything is dedicated to restoring balance and harmony. From the design of the rooms and grounds to the cuisine, spa menu and yoga and meditation classes, this spa haven offers a total package which epitomises the word 'holistic'. While it draws from a combination of time-tested healing remedies of the East and West in its spa programmes, its focus is on Ayurveda, augmented by aromatherapy and modern spa technology.

The spa occupies some 1,950 sq m (21,000 sq ft) of space, with a plethora of

treatments to purify and soothe. Ayurveda, an Indian healing system with 5,000 years of curative history, not only addresses ailments but prevents ill health and preserves well-being. Because it treats the person as a whole, equilibrium between the mind and body can be realised. Spa therapies are complemented by yoga and meditation classes to encourage total well-being.

FACTS	**ROOMS**	70 Deluxe Rooms • 3 Deluxe Suites • 1 Ananda Suite
	FOOD	The Restaurant: Ayurvedic, Asian and Western • The Pavilion: light snacks • The Winter Garden: Asian and Continental • The Palace Lounge: high tea • The Poolside: snacks and juices • The Hill Theatre: dinner shows
	FEATURES	yoga • meditation • beauty salon • meditation pavilions • fitness centre • billiard room • library • nature walks • golf course
	BUSINESS	boardrooms • amphitheatre • Viceregal Hall
	NEARBY	Rajaji and Chilla national parks • elephant safaris • white water rafting • angling
	CONTACT	The Palace Estate, Narendra Nagar, District Tehri-Garhwal, Uttaranchal 249175 • telephone: +91.13.7822 7500 • facsimile: +91.13.7822 7550 • email: sales@anandaspa.com • website: www.anandaspa.com

PHOTOGRAPHS COURTESY OF ANANDA IN THE HIMALAYAS.

The Oberoi Cecil, Shimla

In the early 19th century, the British used to flock to a site 2,134 m (7,000 ft) up the Himalayas, seeking refuge from the searing Indian summers. So popular was this spot that they soon claimed it as their own, establishing it as a hill station in 1830.

The Oberoi Cecil sits proudly at this site today. Its façade may have changed, but like the British hill station that it was before, the hotel continues to act as a sanctuary—a place of rest and comfort—for all who visit.

Built in 1884 and fully restored in 1997, the hotel is located in Shimla, the gateway to the Himalayas. The Oberoi Cecil's classic design has impressed its guests over the years, and continues to do so today. It has a certain charm and elegance which time cannot diminish. Polished wood panelling, carved pillars, sparkling chandeliers, fireplaces, thick carpets and colonial-era furnishings recreate the grandeur of the British Raj.

Many of the hotel's 79 rooms and suites offer spectacular views through large picture windows so that guests can wake up to a panorama of snow-capped peaks, deep

THIS PAGE (CLOCKWISE FROM TOP):
The Oberoi Cecil is set in the lush hills of Shimla; the interiors have been carefully restored to reflect their colonial origins; each room offers views of the surrounding mountains and valleys.
OPPOSITE: Take a dip in the hotel's heated swimming pool to keep the chilly evenings at bay.

valleys and verdant green hills. For a little more space, guests may prefer a Deluxe Room or a Premium Room instead. Also an option are the Executive Suites, which feature a separate living room and walk-in wardrobes. Those who want only the best will opt for the elegantly appointed Deluxe Suite, which comes with a separate living room and bedroom, and a dressing area with a walk-in closet. A private balcony makes this option all the more enticing.

The Oberoi Cecil's old-world charm is also apparent in its dining room, which serves European and Asian fare. Regular thematic evenings celebrate the Indian and colonial heritage of the hotel. If the weather is good, guests may opt to enjoy a light meal outdoors in the Cedar Garden, where they can take in the view and enjoy the crisp mountain air.

The Oberoi Cecil is a hotel for all seasons: guests enjoy air-conditioning in summer, and in winter, the hotel is heated.

This extends to the swimming pool, which is also heated. And each time you take a dip in it, bear in mind one little fact: the pool is one of the highest-located in the world!

Guests make the most of the stunning vistas around them with treks or horseback rides into the mountains. Lakkar Bazaar, the local market, is ideal for souvenir hunters, as is The Mall, Shimla's famous promenade. Also within minutes of The Oberoi Cecil are interesting sites such as the historic Viceregal Lodge and scenic Jakhoo Hill.

FACTS

ROOMS	22 Superior Rooms • 27 Premium Rooms • 22 Deluxe Rooms • 3 Executive Suites • 5 Deluxe Suites
FOOD	dining room: European and Asian • Cedar Garden: light meals
DRINK	The Lobby Lounge • bar
FEATURES	The Oberoi Spa by Banyan Tree • pool • gym • billiards • activities centre
BUSINESS	wireless Internet access • conference rooms • AV equipment
NEARBY	The Mall • Lakkar Bazaar • The Viceregal Lodge • Jakhoo Hill • golf • trekking • horseback riding • fruit orchards • hot springs
CONTACT	Chaura Maidan, Shimla 171004, Himachal Pradesh • telephone: +91.177.2804 848 • facsimile: +91.177.2811 024 • email: reservations@oberoi-cecil.com • website: www.oberoicecil.com

PHOTOGRAPHS COURTESY OF THE OBEROI CECIL, SHIMLA.

Wildflower Hall, Shimla in the Himalayas

Located 2,600 m (8,250 ft) above sea level and nestled amidst cedar and pine forests, Wildflower Hall, in the Himalayas, is a luxury resort renowned for its breathtaking views, superb facilities and attention to service.

Without fail, every visitor who comes to the resort is awestruck by the view. And who would not be? Deep, beautiful valleys, snow-capped mountains and verdant landscapes of flowering plants and fragrant trees surround the property.

Rising just six storeys high, Wildflower Hall is a picturesque resort reminiscent of the days of the British Raj. Its façade is finished with traditional *dhajji*, and balconies feature on its upper floors. Descriptions such as 'quaint', 'old world' and 'charming' are common, and totally apt.

The extravagant interior of Wildflower Hall reflects the best of colonial British style, with dark wood panelling, thick carpets, original artworks and artefacts, fireplaces, elegant furniture and crystal chandeliers.

This extends to the resort's rooms and suites. Every room comes with polished teak floors, hand-knotted rugs, plush carpets and personalised butler service. The Executive Suites have a separate living room with a fireplace, while the impressive Lord Kitchener Suite, named after the most famous Commander-in-Chief of India, offers a four-poster bed in the master suite and a second bedroom, making it a popular choice with families. The magnificent scenery around the resort can be admired from all 85 rooms and suites, restaurants and public areas.

Dining at Wildflower Hall is always a treat. At The Restaurant, guests can savour an array of local and Continental dishes. For drinks after dinner, head to The Cavalry Bar, where a range of fine wines and spirits await.

Though it may seem an unlikely place to hold a business meeting or retreat, the inspiring landscape surrounding Wildflower Hall can bring out the best in business executives. The hotel has four conference rooms which can accommodate up to 100 people in various capacities. When the work is done, adventure seekers can follow meandering paths into the valleys and mountains, or set off on a river rafting expedition over the Sutlej River, while others may opt for a romantic picnic in the hotel's expansive surroundings.

If time permits, guests may choose to embark on a trek into the dense forests surrounding the property, which are populated by a variety of wildlife. Trekkers have reported sightings of jackals, deer, and on the rare occasion, the leopard, as well as numerous bird species such as the blue magpie.

PHOTOGRAPHS COURTESY OF WILDFLOWER HALL, SHIMLA IN THE HIMALAYAS.

FACTS		
ROOMS	81 Deluxe Rooms • 3 Executive Suites • 1 Lord Kitchener Suite	
FOOD	The Restaurant: Continental and local	
DRINK	The Cavalry Bar	
FEATURES	The Oberoi Spa by Banyan Tree • pool • gym • sauna and jacuzzi • card room • billiards • library • tennis	
BUSINESS	Internet access • business centre • boardrooms and conference rooms	
NEARBY	river rafting • mountain biking • horseback riding • trekking • archery • golf • ice skating	
CONTACT	Chharabra, Shimla 171012, Himachal Pradesh • telephone: +91.177.2648 585 • facsimile: +91.177.2648 686 • email: reservations@wildflowerhall.com • website: www.oberoihotels.com	

Jammu + Kashmir

Pakistan

Himachal
Pradesh

Punjab

Haryana

Uttaranchal

Delhi

Rajasthan

Uttar
Pradesh

Madhya
Pradesh

Maharashtra

Goa

Karnataka

Andhra
Pradesh

Tamil Nadu

Nepal

People's Republic of China

eastindia

Sikkim

Bhutan

Arunachal
Pradesh

Assam

Nagaland

Meghalaya

Manipur

Bihar

Bangladesh

Tripura

Mizoram

Jharkhand

West
Bengal

Myanmar

Chhattisgarh

Orissa

> The Oberoi Grand, Kolkata
> The Park, Kolkata

Thailand

Bay of Bengal

Andaman
+ Nicobar Islands

the tale of a capital

Well until the 1960s, the people who loved Kolkata and lived there referred to Delhi as that 'boring village' up north. Never mind that Delhi was the seat of some of the greatest empires that ruled the country. Never mind that Delhi boasted some of the finest monuments and architectural marvels as well as universities and centres of learning in the world. This snobbery and deprecation of India's capital by the people of 'Cal', as they affectionately called their city, stemmed from several things. Kolkata was—and is—India's largest metropolis. It was, until 1911, the nation's capital, when Delhi was built and the seat of government shifted there. Kolkata was India's most vibrant city. It had a modern tram system, like that of London,and indeed, parts of it resemble London—the Victorian and Georgian architecture, cobbled streets straight out of a Charles Dickens novel, nightclubs with crooners singing the blues, and streets with names like Park, Camac and Middleton. And like the Thames, the great Hooghly River, a massive waterway full of tugs, schooners and fishing boats, journeys through the city, at one point under Howrah Bridge, flowing into the Bay of Bengal, one of the largest estuaries in the world. More than two million people cross the bridge daily.

The port city of Kolkata, capital of West Bengal, could not have been better suited to be India's former capital. Because of its hinterland and abundance of natural and intellectual wealth, it was known as the 'Ruhr of India'. It lacked nothing. It had one of the world's finest ports, a shipping industry, airports, inland waterway transport, coal, iron ore, cotton, timber, paddy cultivation, steel mills, tea gardens and more. It was home to prosperous European and British companies, including firms like Duncan Brothers, Shaw Wallace, Averys, Benson's Advertising and Imperial Tobacco, and banks like Grindlays. James Morris writes in *Pax Britannica*, 'In the evenings, the richer British Box-wallahs (executives) emerged in top hats and frock coats to promenade in the Maidaan (the great expanse of greenery in the middle of town, not unlike Manhattan's Central Park or London's Hyde Park), driving steadily here and there in broughams, hansoms and victories, exchanging bows and transient assessments.'

PAGE 46: The tea plantations of the easterns hills under heavy morning cloud.

THIS PAGE: The stately Marble Palace, built in 1835, is an art gallery with a prized collection of Chinese and Japanese porcelain.

OPPOSITE: Howrah Bridge is a cantilever truss bridge built in 1943.

Fun, commerce and trade were only some of the things Kolkata's snobs boasted about. Their real sense of individuality came from their distinct Bengali culture and language. As Trevor Fishlock wrote in *India File*, 'Calcutta is the Left Bank with its café society, Bohemian airs, political arguments and love of gossip.' This is the land of Nobel laureates—poet Rabindranath Tagore, Mother Teresa, economist Amartya Sen, world-renowned English classicist Nirad Chowdhuri, and Satyajit Ray, whose *Pather Panchali* (the first of three 'Apu' films) is hailed across the world as a classic. West Bengal led the Hindu reform and renaissance movements of the 19th century—the Bramho Samaj and Arya Samaj—and its Vedic scholars, Swami Ramakrishna, Swami Vivekananda and Sri Aurobindo stunned the world with their expositions on philosophy and religion. Its patriots such as Subhas Chandra Bose inspired and led India's struggle for independence from the British in the first half of the 20th century.

With this glorious heritage, the Bengali chauvinist may well have considered Delhi, India's capital, a bore. But the inhabitants of Delhi probably had the last laugh as Kolkata began a commercial decline in the 1960s. Massive labour unrest and the trade union movement that often turned violent drove capital and professionals out of the state, and the city was plunged into an economic crisis that exacerbated poverty and unemployment. Many Indians dubbed it a 'dying city'. Kolkata is overcrowded and with the city's poorest inhabitants sometimes dwelling right on the pavement, the city can be a high-voltage culture shock for those visiting for the first time. But it is not a dying city. The city and the state are now beginning to recover because of the Leftist government's new liberalised economic policies and structural reforms which are designed to draw both foreign and domestic investment to the state. And the turnaround has begun. Kolkata's new underground railway system is today the envy of other Indian cities. Multinational Indian companies such as Tata Steel and several IT firms are making new investments in West Bengal. The beautification of the city's riverfront has begun as well, starting with construction of the Floatel—the first floating star-category hotel in India.

the pull of the east

In spite of all this, Kolkata is too dynamic, diverse, historical and wonderfully scenic to be judged only by the parameters of commerce and economics. It exudes a singular vibrancy. The city is still the jewel of India's eastern region in which Lord Gautama Buddha was born and attained Enlightenment. The east includes the states of West Bengal, Assam, Bihar and Orissa—the coastal state with its renowed Sun Temple and glorious coastline. Many consider this area to be of great spiritual and intellectual significance, citing its numerous temples and historical places of study.

Kolkata is not only India's largest metropolis but also one of the largest cities in the world, its greater area sprawling across some 102 km (63 miles). Established as a British trading post in the 17th century, the city grew rapidly, becoming, after London, the second city of the British Empire. Its glory is still reflected in the buildings of Chowringhee and Clive Street, re-christened Jawaharlal Nehru Road and Netaji

THIS PAGE (FROM LEFT): Indian dancers rehearse for the festival of Durga Puja; the Kali temple of Dakshineshwar is a popular site with worshippers and tourists.

OPPOSITE (FROM TOP): A statue of Queen Victoria at the hall built in her memory; a vendor prepares sweet treats at one of the city's bazaars.

Subhash Road. It is a city which leaves nobody indifferent. It is fascinating, effervescent, and teeming with life, people and cultures. On first impact it can be confusing, even terrifying, as visitors attempt to manoeuvre the streets along with rickshaws pulled by men, numerous cars, brightly painted lorries and trolley buses, all while street vendors try to grab their attention with high-decibel cries. But soon the traveller becomes intrigued as Dominique Lapierre's *The City of Joy* emerges from the cacophony and chaos.

a tourist mecca

The 3-km-long (1.9-mile-long) Maidaan in central Kolkata is an inner-city greenbelt where people stroll, toddlers learn to take their first steps, and lovers cuddle on benches or beautifully maintained lawns. Around it are a number of sights worth exploring. A building you simply cannot miss while there is the sprawling, white marble Victoria Memorial Hall, built by the British in 1921 as a tribute to Queen Victoria. It houses a collection of Indian art and artefacts. The building is illuminated every night, giving it an otherworldly glow. At nearby Jawaharlal Nehru Road is the Indian Museum, the oldest museum in Asia. Established in 1814, it is an eloquent expression of classical architecture—a Corinthian portico and proscenium arch-style auditorium— and houses the gargantuan collection of the Asiatic Society. Also in the vicinity of the Maidaan are St Paul's Cathedral, built in 1847 as a Gothic imitation of England's Canterbury Cathederal, and the Birla Planetarium, one of the largest in the country.

Across the river sprawls the Indian Botanic Garden, laid out in 1786. A favourite haunt with tourists is the massive 250-year-old banyan tree which sprawls over 400 m (1,312 ft). Also a highlight is the temple of Dakshineshwar, honouring the goddess Kali, who is associated with the goddess Durga. Every September/October Kolkata's streets explode with Mardi Gras-like colour, dance, food, music and revelry, celebrating the festival of Durga Puja. Terracotta images of the goddess are placed on thousands of floats, carted across the city, and immersed in the Hooghly at sunset.

wine, dine and shop

There is plenty of good food, dozens of luxury hotels, and all sorts of entertainment to keep visitors occupied in Kolkata, from golf to bowling, boat cruises and nightclubs. For Bengali cuisine, some of the better eateries are Saruchi, run by the All-Bengal Women's Union, a no frills 'what-mother-makes-at-home' establishment, and the tower-top restaurant, Charnock's, offering jumbo shrimp from the Bay of Bengal and a splendid bird's eye view of the city. Wherever you eat in the hundreds of upmarket or humble local restaurants, whether it is Indian, Oriental, multi-cuisine, Mughlai or South Indian, do not forget to try the *mishti doi* (sweet, rich yoghurt).

Among the hottest nightclubs is Tantra at The Park, Kolkata, featuring chic décor, fashion shows and a string of celebrity guests.

Shoppers should make a beeline for several speciality locales: delicate fabrics in Burra Bazaar, exquisite gold jewellery in B. B. Ganguly Street, handmade Chinese shoes at Bentinck Street, fine porcelain at the Old China Bazaar, and just about everything at New Market, which is actually Kolkata's oldest market.

the marvels yonder

If you want to take a quick break from the bustle and heat of Kolkata, hop on a plane or boat from Kolkata to Port Blair in the Andaman and Nicobar Islands for a complete change of pace and scenery. These are verdant, blue-skied islands in the Bay of Bengal with sleepy lagoons, picnic huts and friendly fisherfolk. To beat the heat, use Kolkata as your gateway to Darjeeling for an experience in the mighty Himalayas.

Farther east are the states of Assam and Meghalaya. Assam, a rainy state, is recognised as one of the world's largest and most productive tea-producing areas and is home to some formidable wildlife. Assam's capital, Guwahati, lies along the banks of one of India's mightiest rivers, the Brahmaputra. From here, visitors can access many of the state's interesting sights, including wildlife reserves such as Manas, known for its

great tigers, and Kaziranga, often described by visitors as one of the most imposing reserves in the world and comparable to the best in eastern and southern Africa. It is also home to the Indian one-horned rhinoceros.

Bordering Assam to the north is the mountain kingdom of Bhutan, and further east lies the state of Meghalaya (meaning 'land of the clouds'), home to the Khasis and Garos, who make up the majority of the population. Meghalaya is one of only three Indian states to have a Christian majority. Shillong, the capital, is a modern city with English-medium schools, churches and convents. The state is considered off the beaten path, but those who visit once easily come under the spell cast by its many waterfalls, including Noh Kalikai, Mawsmai and Imilchang Dare, and abundance of verdant hills. From its highest spot, Shillong Peak, a scenic picnic area 1,965 m (6,467 ft) above sea level, visitors are treated to panoramic views of the countryside and surrounding hills. Meghalaya is where you will find one of the best golf courses in India, Shillong Golf Course, set in a valley amidst pine trees and rhododendrons at an altitude of 1,585 m (5,200 ft). The roaring monsoon months (end June to September) may keep you indoors, but Meghalaya's rainy season is something worth remembering.

Moving down south, below West Bengal, is the state of Orissa (the ancient kingdom of Kalinga, where Emperor Asoka embraced non-violence and Buddhism after

THIS PAGE: Explore Kaziranga National Park on the back of an elephant.

OPPOSITE (CLOCKWISE FROM TOP LEFT): Hindus express their devotion to gods and deities by erecting shrines; tuck into delicious Indian cuisine at the bazaars; a fruit-seller sorts oranges at a local market.

THIS PAGE: *A wheel on the chariot of the Sun God at the Sun Temple of Konark.*

OPPOSITE: *Lingaraja Temple is one of the largest and most architecturally evolved structures in Bhubaneshwar.*

winning a bloody war) along the Bay of Bengal. It has a rich history of artistic endeavour, ranging from *odissi* classical dance, to music, and the creations of its artisans and sculptors, including forms such as *pipili* (appliqué work) and silver filigree ornamental work from Cuttack. Like Chennai in the south, the state's capital, Bhubaneshwar, is also a great temple town. Together with two other temple towns in the state, Konark and Puri, Bhubaneshwar is part of the east's Golden Triangle tour circuit. The sacred Bindusagar Lake in old Bhubaneshwar was once ringed by 7,000 temples, of which 500 still survive. Puri is a coastal town south of Bhubaneshwar and is among the four holiest Hindu cities in India. It is now also being developed as an eco-friendly beach resort. Go to Puri in June or July when it is possible to participate in one of India's greatest festivals, the spectacular Rath Yatra or 'Car Festival', when millions of pilgrims gather to pay homage to the images of the deity Jagannath (a form of Lord Krishna), drawn on massive wooden chariots pulled by thousands of people. In fact, the etymological source of the English word 'juggernaut' is the deity 'Jagannath'.

In isolated splendour, as if rising out of the sand dunes rimming the blue waters of the bay, the 13th-century black granite Sun Temple of Konark—sometimes called 'the Black Pagoda'—marks not just Orissa's but India's supreme triumph in the field of temple architecture. It was built as a chariot for the Sun God, complete with wheels and horses. This World Heritage Site is accessible from both Puri and Bhubaneshwar.

Another eastern state, but northwest of West Bengal, is Bihar. This is where the Buddha attained Enlightenment under the Bodhi tree 2,500 years ago. The state is also home to the ruins of Nalanda, a celebrated centre of Buddhist learning from the 5th to 12th centuries. This great seat of learning attracted students not only from India but also Tibet, China, Korea, Japan and Indonesia. According to Chinese pilgrim-scholar Hiuen-Tsang, writing in the first half of the 7th century, the campus had 10,000 monks and students, and 2,000 teachers, plus a library of nine million manuscripts. With so much history behind it, it is no wonder the east is considered the cradle of India's spiritual and religious development.

...the cradle of India's spiritual and religious development.

The Oberoi Grand, Kolkata

Located in Chowringhee, the heart of Kolkata's commercial and shopping district, The Oberoi Grand is reminiscent of India's colonial past. Its entrance is a grand statement, with classical finishes and strong lines complemented by swaying palm trees and plants.

The interiors of the hotel, with high ceilings, stately columns and muted lighting, portray an elegance and style distinct to Oberoi hotels and resorts. The lobby is a sight to behold with its unique green marble floor, and design details splendidly set off by clever lighting, refreshing floral blooms and comfortable furnishings.

Graceful living extends to the beautifully appointed guestrooms and suites. The Superior Rooms enjoy views of the city, while the Deluxe Rooms overlook the pool. The three spacious Executive Suites are

THIS PAGE (FROM TOP): The Oberoi Grand's stately entrance hints at the lavish interiors guests can expect; the elegant lobby is reminiscent of a bygone era.

OPPOSITE (FROM LEFT): The Deluxe Suite has a comfortable living room with teak floors, leading to a separate dining area; with a four-poster bed, large work table and DVD player, the Deluxe Room is ideal for both work and relaxation.

...these suites offer guests the option of hosting small in-room cocktail parties or meetings.

popular with business travellers. With two balconies as well as a separate living room, these suites offer guests the option of hosting small in-room cocktail parties or meetings.

The Deluxe Suites are all-time favourites, designed for those who appreciate exclusive living. There are three balconies which overlook the courtyard and pool, and a generous drawing/dining room.

The restaurants at the hotel see a sizeable crowd on a regular basis, thanks to the culinary skills of the chefs. La Terrasse is a French brasserie-style restaurant serving a variety of international cuisine in a sumptuous buffet spread. Baan Thai, one of Kolkata's premier Thai restaurants, offers an authentic taste of Thailand.

After a day spent negotiating a tough contract, or shopping for the city's best buys, a visit to The Oberoi Spa is a great way to unwind. Here, Thai-trained therapists will knead away the tightness in your muscles, and help to induce a wonderful sense of bliss. The extensive spa menu includes a range of holistic therapies, from Ayurvedic treatments to aromatherapy, and Thai, Balinese and Indian massages. Guests may opt for a complete package covering everything from head to toe.

Exercise enthusiasts will appreciate the well-equipped gym and outdoor pool, while the nearby golf course, stables, and squash and tennis facilities offer more options.

In the hotel's vicinity are many places of historical interest. Two good stops in particular are Fort William and Kalighat Temple. The latter is an important temple of Kali, the goddess from whom Kolkata supposedly took its name.

FACTS

ROOMS	43 Superior Deluxe Rooms • 87 Premium Rooms • 74 Deluxe Rooms • 3 Junior Suites • 3 Executive Suites • 3 Deluxe Suites
FOOD	La Terrasse: international • Baan Thai: Thai
DRINK	Chowringhee Bar • Poolside Bar • Tea Lounge
FEATURES	The Oberoi Spa by Banyan Tree • pool • fitness centre • beauty salon
BUSINESS	wireless Internet access • meeting rooms • business centre • ballroom
NEARBY	Victoria Memorial Hall • The Maidaan • Ochterlony Monument • Kalighat Temple • Fort William • horseback riding • golf • tennis • squash • shopping
CONTACT	15 Jawaharlal Nehru Road, Kolkata 700013, West Bengal • telephone: +91.33.2249 2323 • facsimile: +91.33.2249 3229 • email: reservations@oberoi-cal.com • website: www.oberoihotels.com

PHOTOGRAPHS COURTESY OF THE OBEROI GRAND, KOLKATA.

The Park, Kolkata

Located in the city's bustling centre, The Park, Kolkata is right at the doorstep of the commercial and entertainment districts.

The hotel is a particular favourite with those who appreciate the finer things in life—elegant interiors, contemporary décor and state-of-the-art technology. Every guestroom showcases a mix of architectural elements drawn from India's colonial past and its vision for the future.

The Residence, The Park's all-suite floor, offers guests a beautiful home away from home, complete with 24-hour butler service. Designed to pamper, the suite's amenities include sophisticated DVD and sound systems and luxurious four-feature bathrooms with jacuzzis. In addition to this, guests have exclusive use of The Residence Lounge for dining or small meetings.

Zen, the hotel's Thai and Sichuan restaurant, is popular for a host of reasons— its black-and-white interior, artistic lighting, impactful wall art and delectable choices being just a few of them.

Saffron is an innovative restaurant which serves sumptuous contemporary Indian cuisine. The chefs have created dishes which are inspired by the diversity of Indian culture and its rich culinary traditions.

Though The Park offers many after-dinner distractions, by far the most popular is Tantra. At 465 sq m (5,000 sq ft), this nightclub offers ample space to show off the latest dance moves. Two levels with different characteristics allow guests to choose the best spot to people-watch or enjoy the pulsating energy permeating the club. Though the atmosphere changes according

to daily themes, Tantra remains the preferred hangout of young executives and the jetset.

New to the scene is Roxy, the city's only cocktail bar. The 1960s-inspired design, with spacious interiors, rounded edges and plush upholstery, make it a retro hit. The menu of wines and cocktails is admirable, but the Champagne mixes are definitely the drinks to try, as are the Martinis.

Someplace Else is yet another nightclub at The Park, one which has retained its popularity for over 10 years. Every evening,

the club's many guests enjoy 'live' music performed by some of the city's best bands.

Guests who want to bring home a little memento of India should head to The Box, where a selection of handcrafted items, exquisite gifts and unique artefacts await.

The Park, Kolkata's location makes sightseeing a breeze. Victoria Memorial Hall, built by the British early in the 20th century, is in the vicinity, as is St Paul's Cathedral, built in 1839. Other places of interest include the Indian Museum and Birla Planetarium.

THIS PAGE (FROM TOP): Tantra pleases with its chic décor; The Atrium Café serves an international menu at all hours of the day and night.

OPPOSITE (CLOCKWISE FROM BELOW): The well-appointed Deluxe Room exudes contemporary style; the 'hip' factor is reflected in the black-and-white checked bedspread, distinctive wall art and circular mirror; the predominance of light brown, white and beech enhances the sleek and spacious feel of the rooms.

FACTS		
ROOMS	89 Deluxe Rooms • 43 Luxury Rooms • 17 The Residence Suites	
FOOD	Zen: Thai and Sichuan • The Atrium Café: international • Saffron: Indian	
DRINK	Tantra • Someplace Else • Roxy	
FEATURES	The Residence Lounge • pool • spa • fitness centre • gift shop	
BUSINESS	Internet access • meeting room • banquet facilities	
NEARBY	Royal Calcutta Golf Club and Tollygunge Club • Oxford Bookstore • Victoria Memorial Hall • St Paul's Cathedral • National Library • Eden Gardens • Indian Museum • Birla Planetarium	
CONTACT	17 Park Street, Kolkata 700016, West Bengal • telephone: +91.33.2249 9000 • facsimile: +91.33.2249 4000 • email: resv.cal@theparkhotels.com • website: www.theparkhotels.com	

PHOTOGRAPHS COURTESY OF THE PARK, KOLKATA.

where it all began

India's heartland, beginning where the Himalayan region ends, spawned its ancient Sanskrit culture. Very broadly, it comprises the states of Haryana, Punjab, the fertile Indo-Gangetic plains of Uttar Pradesh, Madhya Pradesh and India's capital, Delhi.

Delhi stands at the western end of the plains, bordered on one side by the state of Uttar Pradesh and on the other by the state of Haryana. It covers an area of 1,483 sq km (573 sq miles) and has a population of 13.8 million.

Historically, he who ruled from Delhi was best able to control the subcontinent. Strategic routes from Central Asia and the high valleys of Afghanistan are accessible from here. It is from these regions that Delhi's first conquerors came, using this ancient settlement which has been around since 1200 BC as a base from which they could pillage and plunder the wealthy areas of the Indo-Gangetic plains. But the battle for actual control of Delhi began in the 11th century, with tribes and conquerers from Central Asia fighting for supremacy. They included the dreaded Tamerlane, Emir of Samarkand and conqueror of Persia, Afghanistan and Mesopotamia, who sacked Delhi in 1398 and took home 120 elephants as loot.

Mughal control of Delhi began in the early 16th century with Emperor Babar, a former overlord of Samarkand and a descendant of both Tamarlane and Genghis Khan. Following Babar's death in 1530, his son Humayun ascended the throne. His great-grandson was Shah Jahan, the emperor behind the Taj Mahal.

two for the price of one

Delhi is really two cities, one being New Delhi, with its boulevards, spacious lime-washed bungalows and Victorian architecture, much of which was erected in the early 20th century when the British moved India's capital from Kolkata to New Delhi in 1911. The second, Old Delhi, was the 17th-century walled city of Shahjahanabad, with city gates and narrow alleys built by the Mughal rulers. The ultimate symbol of Mughal power is the imposing Red Fort, or Lal Qila. Its watchtowers rise to 18 m

PAGE 62: Candles float down the holy Ganges River.

THIS PAGE: Delhi's India Gate is a 42-m-high (138-ft-high) memorial to Indian soldiers.

OPPOSITE: Completed in 1648, the sandstone Red Fort is one of Emperor Shah Jahan's architectural legacies.

(60 ft), and its perfectly shaped ramparts and embattlements extend over 2.5 km (1.6 miles), overlooking the Yamuna River. Old Delhi is also synonymous with temples, bazaars, the famous street shopping area known as Chandni Chowk, and Jama Masjid—India's largest mosque, with a courtyard that can accommodate 20,000 people. It was built by the most romantic of the Mughals, Emperor Shah Jahan.

In contrast, New Delhi is a more spaciously planned city of wide, tree-lined streets, parks and fountains, designed primarily by British architect Edwin Lutyens. The edifices of the Raj, some built with red sandstone, are clustered on and around Raisina Hill. Among these is Rashtrapati Bhavan, the Indian presidential palace which was once home to the British Viceroy—a magnificent rose garden stands within its compound. South and North Block are New Delhi's Whitehall, from where all important government departments function. Parliament House, circular and colonnaded, is part of this cluster. Legislative sessions are often raucous and theatrical. For a front row seat, visitor passes can be obtained from the office on Raisina Road.

when past is present

On the accommodation front, Delhi has everything, from five-star hotels comparable to the best anywhere in the world to budget joints costing no more than a few dollars a night. Bargains are not to be expected at Delhi's top hotels, but you will get first-rate service, enjoy the convenience of 24-hour coffee shops, and have access to an extensive range of amenities. The two main centres for accommodation are Paharganj (budget), near New Delhi Railway Station, and Janpath (budget and mid-range), on the southern side of Connaught Place.

Getting around to see the sights is not a hassle. Deluxe air-conditioned buses can be arranged at any of the hotels. Taxis are a telephone call away. And for the more adventurous, there are the three-wheelers. Fuelled by compressed natural gas, these auto-rickshaws are one of the cheapest mode of transportation and can manoeuvre their way through Delhi's horrendous traffic jams with admirable alacrity.

Sightseeing can begin anywhere. Evidence of Hindu, Mughal, British and post-independence India exist side by side. To describe Delhi's tourist spots and monuments would take volumes, but some examples should suffice here.

Ancient India has left a marvellous relic on Maharani Jhansi Road, the Ashoka Pillar (3rd century BC) on which are inscribed, as Emperor Ashoka decreed, some of the tenets of Buddhism which he embraced. If you want to see Hindu India at its creative and scientific best, visit the sandstone-and-marble Jantar Mantar, the observatory built by Maharaja Jai Singh II in 1724. Hindu India is also represented by thousands of temples, the most modern being the Lakshmi Narayan Temple built by the Birla industrialist family—the Birlas also built India's first motor car. Examples of pre-Mughal Delhi can be seen in the semi-forested, rocky Mehrauli area, whose most famous landmark is the 73-m-tall (240-ft-tall), five-storeyed Qutb Minar, or 'Victory Tower', commemorating the victory of the Turkish Slave Dynasty ruler Qutb-ud-din Aibak over a Hindu king in 1199. The area is now a garden complex with eateries surrounded by a huge flower bazaar. There is even a fancy nightclub in the vicinity.

THIS PAGE: Lakshmi Narayan Temple is an Orissan-style structure dedicated to the goddess of wealth.

OPPOSITE: Jantar Mantar features a large sundial and instruments which can predict eclipses.

THIS PAGE: *The towering Qutb Minar has five storeys, each with a projecting balcony.*

OPPOSITE (FROM TOP): *Jama Masjid's alternating strips of red sandstone and white marble add to its striking appearance; explore the sights on a three-wheeler.*

Also within this complex is India's first mosque, Quwwat-ul-Islam Masjid ('Might of Islam Mosque'), built in 1193 by Qutb-ud-din Aibak as well.

Mughal Delhi is exemplified by the black-and-white marble-and-red sandstone Humayun's Tomb on Lodi Road. The structure, with its flanking arches, bulbous dome, fountains, central canal and octagonal base plan, was built between 1555 and 1569 by the Emperor's widow Haji Begum.

capital shopping

One of Britain's commercial contributions to Delhi is Connaught Place (CP), also known as Connaught Circle, a ring of colonial arcades surrounding a park, with an 'inner' and 'outer' circle. Until the advent of South Delhi, CP was the entertainment and shopping heart of New Delhi, with restaurants, antique dealers, haberdashers, strip-tease joints, handicrafts shops, travel agents, chemists, general stores, Indian barbecue stalls, elegant cinema halls, coffee shops, bars and budget hotels.

CP still beckons the shopper. It is a good place to browse and buy fabrics, crafts, furniture, pottery, carpets and jewellery, especially at various fixed-priced outlets such as Central Cottage Industries Emporium. CP is also where you can find State Emporiums, a number of state government shops selling authentic products from all around the country, with items ranging from jewellery to curtains, lanterns, shawls, embroidered fabrics, lacquered furniture, musical instruments, and even spices like saffron, cardamom and cloves. For Indian and Nepali antiques and handicrafts, the nearby bungalow-style Sunder Nagar Market is an ideal stop.

If you want to haggle for trinkets and curios, and eat authentic Mughal food in an 'Arabian Nights' atmosphere, Old Delhi's Chandni Chowk, adjacent to Jama Masjid, is the place to be. You will have to get used to being jostled, finding yourself stuck in human traffic jams, and learn to deal with overflowing drains and occasionally having the front tyre of a bicycle going over your shoes. But, if you conquer your claustrophobia and learn to go with the flow, Chandni Chowk will reward you.

yuppie mobility

Outside the world of classic and imperial Delhi with its monuments, museums—including the National Gallery of Modern Art, National Museum, International Dolls Museum, Rail Museum, gardens, markets and bazaars, and its string of bookshops selling every new title, lies yuppie Delhi. This is the creation of the newly moneyed class of builders and exporters, IT entrepreneurs, advertising executives and international bankers. They drive Hondas, Toyotas, Fords, Peugeots and Indian-made Suzukis, Tata and Mahindra recreational vehicles at breakneck speed across the city's notoriously pot-holed roads, and live in high-rise luxury apartments reminiscent of those in Singapore, Hong Kong and New York.

South Delhi's commercial centres like South Extension, Lajpat Nagar, Hauz Khas and Greater Kailash are upmarket shopping and residential districts. Over the last five years, neighbouring Gurgaon's DLF Area has been developing into India's 'millennium city'. Although based in the state of Haryana, it is really Delhi's satellite township and is no more than 25 km (15 miles) away. Commuting is going to become easier with the completion of a superfast 35-km-long (22-mile-long) elevated toll road. Gurgaon's multi-storeyed malls, with cineplexes showing the latest Hollywood and Bollywood releases, are second to none in the world and offer foreign perfumes, toiletries and brands such as Dockers and Levi's at prices lower than in Europe or America. Some of the most happening pubs in Gurgaon are the Buddha Lounge, Buzz, Mojo, Rodeo and Tangerine.

food and fun

There is no shortage of entertainment anywhere in or near Delhi. The Dilli Haat is a 2.4-hectare (6-acre) retreat of landscaped brick and terracotta offering shopping and cuisine from every part of India, and it is now open as a night bazaar. Sports enthusiasts will appreciate the over 15 golf courses and country clubs in and around

THIS PAGE: Delhi's Lodi Gardens are home to the tombs of Sayyid and Lodi rulers.

OPPOSITE (FROM TOP): Master the crowds of Old Delhi to better experience the city's bazaars; whether it is vegetarian or not, Indian or Western, visitors will surely find something to suit their palate.

Delhi to which tourists flock from all over the world, and particularly from Japan and South Korea. Garden restaurants, hotel dining rooms, neighbourhood family joints, malls and bazaars offer Indian, Chinese, Thai, Continental and Japanese food. Clubs, pubs, stylish lounge bars and discos keep the city buzzing at night.

A must-visit infotainment centre is the India Habitat Centre near Lodi Road. A Rockefeller Center-lookalike, the institution is a place for events, book readings, art exhibitions, mini film festivals and debates. It has five restaurants, a multi-cuisine food court, one of the best bar-lounges in the city, a health club, swimming pool and 18 conference halls. Another older institution of a similar nature, but smaller in size, is the India International Centre (IIC) with its world famous reading room and library, quaint annexe pub and dining room overlooking Lodi Gardens. Visitors agree that IIC serves the best lamb chops with homemade mint sauce in the world.

beyond delhi

Delhi is a great starting point for any traveller who wants to explore the central states and submerge himself in an ocean of history, romance and sensuality. These areas are all easily accessed by most modes of transport—air, rail and road—and have plenty of places to stay with prices to suit every pocket.

Start in Haryana, the state that borders Delhi. Travel north on National Highway 1, and within three hours you will reach Kurukshetra, the site of the mother of all wars in 3000 BC, fought for spreading *dharma*. The battle between blood relatives, the Kauravas and Pandavas, is the story behind the Mahabharata, of which the Bhagavad Gita is a section. The Gita, Lord Krishna's battlefield sermon to the warrior Arjuna, contains the essence of the Vedic philosophy of *karma*. The Mahabharata is an epic of over 100,000 couplets, and is the longest poem in the world, about 30 times longer than John Milton's *Paradise Lost*.

Kurukshetra, 160 km (99 miles) from Delhi, has become more popular with visitors since getting a facelift. It can now host overnight guests in clean, comfortable tourist

accommodations. Besides, the national highway is now a modern, convenient expressway with motels, petrol stations, fast-food joints, emergency services, as well as the traditional Indian *dhabas* (roadside eateries serving piping hot vegetarian and non-vegetarian dishes cooked in the open).

Kurukshetra's holy temples and water tanks are an edifying experience. The Brahmasarovar is the largest of these tanks. Hindus revere it as the cradle of civilisation. It is believed that Lord Brahma, creator of the universe, conceived the Earth here.

En route to Kurukshetra, along the same highway, is the city of Panipat where, beginning in the 16th century, armies fought three bloody battles for control of Delhi. In 1526, Babar defeated the ruling Delhi Sultanate and established the Mughal Empire that dominated India for the next 300 years.

Panipat is one of India's hubs for the manufacture of rugs, textiles, drapes and bedcovers which are exported worldwide.

why agra

Agra, located in the state of Uttar Pradesh, is actually 200 km (124 miles) south of Delhi. You can reach it by road or by using the excellent train services, in less than three hours. Agra is India's most famous destination thanks to the Taj Mahal, the 17th-century architectural wonder in marble built by 20,000 workers who toiled for 15 years. The Taj Mahal attracted about 2.5 million visitors in 2004.

Agra is a thrice-blessed city. No other city can boast of three UNESCO World Heritage Sites, the other two—also exemplary Mughal creations—being Agra Fort and the abandoned capital of Fatehpur Sikri. Strict conservation measures have been adopted to protect these sites from the ravages of industrial pollution. In 1993, the Indian Supreme Court ordered the closure of over 200 companies that were not in compliance with air pollution standards. Furthermore, only non-polluting vehicles are allowed in the vicinity of the Taj Mahal, to protect its delicate white marble.

The Taj Mahal may be the world's most beautiful building, but it is also a testament to endless love. Mumtaz Mahal was Emperor Shah Jahan's second wife. In 1631, at age 39, she died while giving birth to their 14th child. The emperor expressed his grief by commissioning the building of the Taj Mahal—the extravagant mausoleum within which their tombs are housed. The building and its gardens are an architectural representation of the Muslim idea of paradise.

Agra's red sandstone fort and palace are just as breathtaking. One could spend a whole day wandering through this monument. When Emperor Akbar chose Agra as his capital, he began construction of the fort. It was his grandson, Shah Jahan, who upgraded the structure to a palace using, once again, white marble. After the Taj Mahal, this is considered to be the second jewel in Agra's architectural crown. Construction began in 1565 and was completed in about eight years. According to chronicler Abul Fazal, the fort originally contained over 500 buildings.

Later, the romantic Shah Jahan was imprisoned in this fort by his own son. His only request was that he be incarcerated in a room with a window facing the Taj Mahal. You can still visit the room and sit at the spot where Shah Jahan sat and gazed at the building within which his beloved Mumtaz was entombed.

Thirty-seven kilometres (23 miles) west of Agra rises Emperor Akbar's dream city, Fatehpur Sikri, also built of red sandstone. It is a maze of courtyards, palaces, passages and ornate doorways that still conjure up images of formidable emperors, their wives and harems, eunuchs, musicians, soldiers and spiritual advisors. The Emperor had planned to have this city as his capital but water shortages forced him to forsake it. Fatehpur Sikri was built between 1571 and 1585. It is a compelling example of the fusion of Mughal and Hindu architecture. Fatehpur Sikri's mosque, known as Jama Masjid, was designed to replicate the holy mosque in Mecca. Entrance to the mosque is through the 54-m-high (177-ft-high) Buland Darwaza.

THIS PAGE: *Explore the well-preserved remains of Fatehpur Sikri.*
OPPOSITE: *Lush Indian fabrics have made their way into the bedrooms, dining rooms and wardrobes of people around the world.*

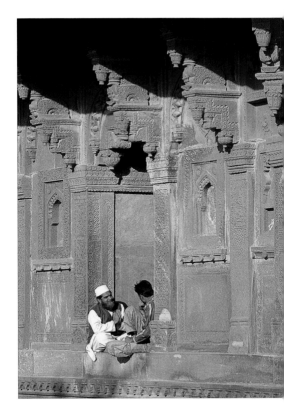

THIS PAGE: *The Taj Mahal's stunning marble screens and inlay work were done by specialists from as far away as Europe.*

OPPOSITE (FROM TOP): *The abandoned city of Fatehpur Sikri is heaven for architecture enthusiasts and history buffs; field workers harvest their crops near Agra.*

Akbar is buried in Sikandra, just 10 km (6.2 miles) from Agra, in an opulent mausoleum which was constructed during the Emperor's lifetime. The structure is a breathtaking fusion of Hindu, Christian, Islamic, Buddhist and Jain motifs.

leather and more

Shoppers will find bargains in every serpentine alley and bazaar of Agra. Marble inlay work comes in the form of plates, trays and vases. Agra's leather goods, bags, jackets, briefcases and even cowboy boots, are the lowest priced in the country and command a huge export market. As for food, Agra has good restaurants and hotels offering the standard American, European or Indian fare. Since tourists often return to Delhi the same day, they usually bring along packed lunches from their respective hotels, but an overnight stay at a good hotel is more fulfilling because you will get to see the Taj Mahal by moonlight, when it shimmers like a precious stone. More time can also be allocated to explore the remains of Fatehpur Sikri.

the refined city

Uttar Pradesh is more than just Agra. It is the hub of the Hindu heartland with a population of more than 150 million. Its capital, Lucknow, a city of gardens and bridges, nestles on a bend of the Gomti River. Its rulers, the Nawabs of Awadh, created their own style of architecture, art and cuisine. Spiritualists and poets of this northern Indian state also propounded an exciting new practice extolling the synthesis of Islamic and Hindu cultures and religion. It was called Sufism. Sufi mysticism was expressed in brilliant, often iconoclastic and irreverent poetry by ascetic poet-saints like Kabir. Their ideas and teachings were liberal and expressed a dynamic humanism.

Lucknow's Nawabs were connoisseurs of fine food—aromatic delicacies created through culinary experimentation with natural scents and spices. They created their own Lucknawi or Awadhi cuisine as distinct from the royal kitchens of the Mughals of Delhi or the sultans of South India. Awadhi cooking aromas waft through the streets of

Lucknow in the evenings. Ask for a variety of kebabs, especially *galoti* and *kakori*, at the hundreds of bazaar eateries. If you want to shop before you eat, look for the famous *chikan* embroidery, *zari* (metallic thread twisted over cotton or silk in a brocade fashion) work, jewellery, perfumes and metalware. Among the great bazaars here are Hazratbal, Aminabad and Chowk.

Lucknow is well known for the cultivated manners of its people and refined urban culture. It continues to promote classical north Indian music and the *kathak* school of dance during the 10-day-long Lucknow Mahotsava in November/December—a tribute to the Nawabs of the Awadh court who patronised these arts.

Lucknow is India's largest Shiite Muslim centre. In fact, Lucknow's Muslims celebrate religious occasions that are more common to Iran than other Sunni communities in the world. Among the outstanding buildings in the city is Bara Imambara, built in 1784. It is primarily a tomb built by Nawab Asaf-ud-Daula, but also houses a mosque which only allows entry to Muslims. Its central hall is one of the world's largest vaulted galleries.

the ancient and the divine

Uttar Pradesh is also home to Varanasi (formerly Benares), reportedly one of the oldest surviving cities in the world, and a contemporary of ancient Babylon, Nineveh and Thebes. Hindus consider this their holiest place because it is believed to be the eternal abode of Lord Shiva or Vishwanath. Mark Twain wrote in 1896 that Varanasi is 'older than history, older than tradition, older even than legend, and looks twice as old as all of them put together.' American poet Allen Ginsberg spent time here living amongst the *sadhus*, meditating, writing and trying to discover the magic of '*om*', the holy sound in Sanskrit scripture.

Here more than anywhere else is the dramatic and palpable evidence of Hinduism's timeless unity with Ganga Mata or Great Mother, the Ganges River. The city's riverfront is a congeries of ghats (steps) in stone and cement that cascade down from the periphery of the town into the river. This is where Hindus come to wash their sins away and to cremate the dead. It is believed dying here offers one *moksha*, or release from the cycle of birth and death. Huge, spired temples, *ashrams*, palaces and Sanskrit schools form an inimitable and unforgettable backdrop to this scene.

While in Varanasi, take a boat ride down the river when evening falls. As the evening prayer (*aarti*) unfolds along the entire stretch of the ghats, temple bells will chime and terracotta lamps will be set afloat down the river in their thousands.

Behind the ghats lie Varanasi's maze of lanes with their bustling bazaars, where shoppers bargain for brocade fabrics, religious art and exotic sweetmeats.

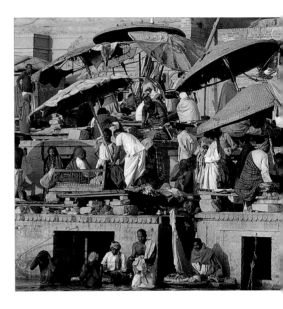

between a rock and a great place

West of Delhi, adjoining Haryana, lies the proud state of Punjab, meaning 'Land of Five Waters', though after partition, just two rivers flow through the state.

Chandigarh, three hours from Delhi by train or via National Highway 1, is the shared capital of both Haryana and Punjab. The town derives its name from the goddess Chandi Devi, whose temple stands 15 km (9 miles) from Chandigarh. Unlike

THIS PAGE: Bathers prepare to wash their sins away in the sacred Ganges.

OPPOSITE (FROM TOP): Varanasi's famous ghats are always a sight to behold; sadhus, ascetic holy men, are a common sight along the ghats.

most modern Indian cities where meticulous medieval, and even ancient planning has given way to urban sprawl, congestion, slums and bad drainage, Chandigarh stands out as an example of calibrated design and purposeful planning. The city's initial plans were drawn in New York by Albert Mayer and Mathew Novicki, but the actual building of the city was supervised by Le Corbusier in 1950.

Residential quarters, defined by sectors, have mandatory green belts and follow blueprints patterned on the geometric logic of juxtaposing people, buildings, space and traffic. Each sector follows the principle of decentralised urbanisation. They are self-contained and self-sufficient units.

Near the centre of the city is the Nek Chand Fantasy Rock Garden, created by a former roads inspector, Nek Chand. He fled his home during the partition of India and Pakistan in 1947 and settled in India's most modern city. His 16-hectare (40-acre) sculptured grounds, containing waterfalls, mini Disney-like castles and pathways, are peopled with thousands of human and animal figures made from broken glass, smashed crockery and earthernware pots, bicycle frames, Coke bottle tops, colourful plastic bangles, slate and tile, and bark, twigs and twine. On one side is a ravine sprouting a thick forest. In addition to the Rock Garden, Nek Chand has permanent installations in Berlin and Washington DC. This popular spot is not to be missed.

triumph of the sikhs

A few hours from Chandigarh is Amritsar, universally revered as the city of the Golden Temple ('Darbar Sahib'), the most sacred of Sikh shrines, with its holy tank called the 'Pool of Nectar'. It epitomises truth, beauty and peace. It started out as a little lake surrounded by a forest, where wandering sages, including Buddha, came and meditated since the beginning of recorded time. Two thousand years after Buddha's time, another philosopher-saint came to live and meditate by the lake. This was Guru Nanak (1469–1539), founder of the Sikh religion. After his passing, his disciples continued to revere the site.

It was the fourth Sikh Guru (Ram Das, 1574–1581), however, who expanded the area and gave a supporting structure to the lake. The Darbar Sahib today stands as the hallowed symbol of the indestructability of the Sikh faith and its openness to all castes and creeds. The evolution of the Golden Temple is inextricably interwined with the history and ideology of Sikhism. Its architecture includes symbols associated with other places of worship. This is an example of the spirit of tolerance and acceptance that the Sikh philosophy propounds. Nearby is the Jallianwala Bagh, where in April 1919, General Dyer opened fire on Indians holding a peaceful demonstration. The place is now a national monument, and its walls bear the bullet marks of this massacre.

endless love

Southeast of Delhi is the state of Madhya Pradesh. Much of its land is hilly and forested, with deep ravines, national parks and rivers flowing westwards into the Arabian Sea and eastwards into the Bay of Bengal. Its capital, Bhopal, founded in 1723 by Dost Mohammed Khan, an Afghan adventurer, drew the attention of the world in 1984 with the Union Carbide gas leak tragedy which killed over 2,500 people and injured thousands more.

THIS PAGE (FROM TOP): **The original Guru Granth Sahib, the Sikh holy text, is housed in the Golden Temple; Nek Chand's Rock Garden will captivate visitors.**

OPPOSITE: **Float down the Ganges in the evening for a different view of the aarti in progress.**

The great tourist attractions of this region are the erotic temple sculptures of Khajuraho—graphic carvings of sexually explicit, embracing and caressing human figures practising just about every carnal pose written about in the Kamasutra, the ancient Indian instruction manual of love-making compiled by the sage Vatsayana between the 2nd and 4th centuries BC. It is based on several earlier Kamashastras ('The Rules of Love') dating to the 7th century BC. On one temple alone, the figures are over 650 in number. This art is pure erotica, distinct from pornography which is associated with an element of sleaze and secrecy.

There are more than 30 sexually explicit temples built under the rule of the Chandela kings in about 900 AD. Archaeologists split them into three distinct groups, Western, Eastern and Southern. The Western group, designated a World Heritage Site, is enclosed within a lush and well-maintained garden. Every year, India's leading dancers, such as Sonal Mansingh, perform on the podium of the Kandariya Mahadev temple that is brilliantly lit for the night-time performance, making the sensuous friezes on the temple walls appear to be in motion too. Today, many honeymooning tourists make a visit to this site, about 150 km (93 miles) south of the town of Jhansi, for special inspiration.

close encounters with nature

Madhya Pradesh is the pulsating centre of India, with more than 30 wildlife sanctuaries, awe-inspiring primeval forests and great waterfalls. The Kanha National Park, a tiger reserve, is also the habitat of the rare barasingha, a swamp deer with up to 14 horns growing out of each main branch. Other parks include Panna, Pench and Bandhavgarh. Here, tigers, leopards, spotted deer, hyenas and nilgai roam free. Bandhavgarh is special as it traverses 32 hills, and a huge fort in this densely forested area is said to have been visited by Lord Rama. As for Pench, it was the site of Kipling's *The Jungle Book*. If bird-watching is what you prefer, try Madhav National Park near Shivpuri, when the best time to visit is between October and February.

THIS PAGE (TOP LEFT AND BELOW):
Whether a mural along the ghats of Varanasi or an erotic sculpture at Khajuraho, Indian art will mesmerise with its colour and form.

OPPOSITE AND THIS PAGE (TOP RIGHT):
Gwalior Fort, northwest of Khajuraho, offers spectacular views from its hilltop location.

Madhya Pradesh is the pulsating centre of India...

Ahilya Fort

Guests at the 250-year-old Ahilya Fort can lay claim to having experienced a truly authentic and royal Indian way of life. Prince Richard Holkar, whose family owns the fort, takes pride in personally playing host to guests—when he is in town, that is.

Dramatically perched on the edge of a cliff, the fort comprises six distinct classes of buildings within which lie well-appointed guestrooms, organic vegetable gardens, picturesque courtyards and terraces, and centuries-old turrets and battlements. From its position high up on the precipice, guests are offered stunning views of the Narmada River and the surrounding areas.

Named after the renowned female ruler Ahilya Bai Holkar, the fort has been preserved with great care in order to maintain the ambience of a bygone era. Though the 1766 structure now has all the modern amenities expected by today's discerning travellers, its distinctive façade and striking architecture have remained largely untouched.

THIS PAGE (CLOCKWISE FROM TOP):
Dining is always a pleasant surprise as the location varies from meal to meal; the stately Ahilya Fort is fronted by the serene Narmada River; embark on a river cruise to see the sights.
OPPOSITE: Enjoy a stunning sunset from any vantage point.

...its distinctive façade and striking architecture have remained largely untouched.

Guests have a choice of 10 beautiful rooms, two luxury tents or a two-bedroom suite. Leveraging on the unrivalled vista presented by the fort's strategic location, rooms come with a private balcony or private garden. If you have any doubts about tent living, they will be immediately dismissed upon viewing the tents at Ahilya Fort. Comfortable and spacious, with en suite bathrooms, these tents promise the ultimate in exclusivity as they are set apart from the other rooms in a private garden. They also overlook the one-km-wide (0.5-mile-wide) river. An abundant use of handloom-woven fabrics gives the interiors a distinctive local air, while ornaments from the 18th century help to re-create an ancient setting.

Dining at Ahilya Fort is always a surprise as meals can be served anywhere within the large compound: breakfast may be enjoyed on a terrace, lunch in a courtyard, and dinner in a garden under the neem trees, or by the pool. As Prince Holkar is a celebrated chef and gourmand, you may be served one of his signature dishes. While there is a menu of sorts, the skilful chefs will happily deal with special requests.

Guests can easily access the weaving centre housed in one of the fort's buildings to watch how the handloom-woven fabrics for which Maheshwar is renowned are made. Other activities include an exploration of the fort and its organic gardens, as well as a boat ride to Baneshwar Temple in the middle of the Narmada River. Ancient Hindu texts have identified the river as the centre of the universe, with the axis between the centre of the earth and the North Pole running straight through the temple. Guests will also enjoy a visit to the romantic, deserted 15th-century town of Mandu.

FACTS

ROOMS	2 Standard Rooms • 8 Superior Rooms • 1 Suite • 2 Luxury Tents
FOOD	Continental and Indian
FEATURES	pool • living room • organic vegetable garden • Nimad traditional massage
BUSINESS	conference hall
NEARBY	Baneshwar Temple • Omkareshwar Temple • Mandu • Maheshwar • Thousand Waterfalls • Dhar Fort • Indore • local handloom houses • farm and vegetable gardens
CONTACT	Maheshwar, Madhya Pradesh 451224 • telephone: +91.11.5155 1575 • facsimile: +91.11.5515 1055 • email: info@ahilyafort.com • website: www.ahilyafort.com

PHOTOGRAPHS COURTESY OF AHILYA FORT.

The Imperial, New Delhi

Located in the cosmopolitan commercial district of Janpath, The Imperial, New Delhi stands out with its majesty and style. It is fitting that a hotel such as this is frequently visited by royalty, dignitaries, artists, celebrities and the international jetset. Undoubtedly one of the finest hotels in Asia, The Imperial has the honour of being a part of the city's original master plan.

Built in 1931, The Imperial features a seamless blend of Victorian, colonial and Art Deco elements. While the massive bronze lions at the entrance are decidedly Victorian, the wrought iron balconies are distinctly 20th-century, and the Art Deco wall panels are an interesting accompaniment to the more sombre colonial style.

Decked out in the best furnishings and amenities sourced from around the world, and complemented by the efficiencies of modern conveniences, The Imperial is the place for gracious living and superb service. All 232 rooms and suites bespeak elegance and distinction, from the lovely interiors to

THIS PAGE (CLOCKWISE FROM TOP): The Spice Route is completely hand-painted with vegetable and flower dyes by mural painters from India's south; the Deco Suites feature muted tones of beige and brown; indulge in a stay at the Royal Imperial Suite.

OPPOSITE: A grand dining experience is assured at 1911.

the spectacular views outside the picture windows. A favourite with the hotel's VIPs is, naturally, the Royal Imperial Suite. Here, guests enjoy the luxury of space, with separate living and dining areas, a private terrace, antique furniture and artworks by Prince Alexis Soltykoff. The hotel's other accommodation options—Imperial Rooms, Heritage Rooms and Suites, Deco Suites and Deluxe Suites, with their different configurations and feel, have garnered their own loyal following. Marble baths and Fragonard toiletries are a standard feature of all these rooms and suites.

Art and fine dining are a highlight at The Imperial, which owns a rare and priceless art collection—'British Art on India'. The finest 18th- and 19th-century paintings, lithographs, sculptures and murals feature in the rooms as well as in the hotel's galleries, corridors and public areas. The Imperial's extensive collection has led to it having the distinction of being known as a 'museum hotel'.

Also noteworthy is the hotel's range of dining options. The 1911 restaurant, a tribute to the establishment of New Delhi as the capital of India in 1911, has an exciting multi-cuisine menu. Guests may dine in three distinct areas: the brasserie, which serves trendy French cuisine for dinner, the bar or the verandah, which overlooks the lawns. Another exceptional choice is The Spice Route, voted one of the top ten restaurants in the world by *Condé Nast Traveler*. Here, diners can savour Southeast Asian cuisine in a restaurant that is visually as stimulating as the food it serves. Daniell's Tavern, the pan-Indian restaurant, is a Raj legacy, while San Gimignano is the capital's best-known fine-dining Italian restaurant.

The hotel is recognised for the complete experience it offers. So whether you are socialising at the Royal Ballroom, strolling in the lush gardens, or visiting nearby temples, you will cherish your stay at The Imperial, New Delhi.

PHOTOGRAPHS COURTESY OF THE IMPERIAL, NEW DELHI.

FACTS		
ROOMS	73 Imperial Rooms • 115 Heritage Rooms • 17 Heritage Suites • 21 Deco Suites • 5 Deluxe Suites • 1 Royal Imperial Suite	
FOOD	1911: multi-cuisine • The Spice Route: Southeast Asian • San Gimignano: Italian • Daniell's Tavern: Indian • 1911 Brasserie: French	
DRINK	Patiala Peg • 1911 Bar	
FEATURES	Six Senses Spa • pool • fitness centre • art galleries • shopping precinct	
BUSINESS	wireless Internet access • business centre • meeting rooms • laptop computers for hire	
NEARBY	Parliament House • President's Palace • museums • theatres • parks • temples	
CONTACT	Janpath, New Delhi 110001 • telephone: +91.11.2334 1234 • facsimile: +91.11.2334 2255 • email: luxury@theimperialindia.com • website: www.theimperialindia.com	

The Oberoi Amarvilās, Agra

A great love cruelly ended, a lifetime of mourning, and a magnificent monument for the world to see—this is the story of the Taj Mahal, an exquisite shrine built by Emperor Shah Jahan in memory of his beloved wife Mumtaz Mahal.

Located 600 m (657 yd) away from the Taj Mahal, The Oberoi Amarvilās offers unparalleled views of this memorial. In particular, guests tend to find themselves struck by the monument's beauty upon entering the lobby, where it is framed by the hotel's grand archways.

Amarvilās itself is also a gem. Architecturally outstanding and lavishly styled, it perfectly complements the grand 16th-century edifices surrounding it.

The name of the hotel, which means 'Eternal Haven', is indicative of its grand stature. The 64 fountains, serene pools, lush gardens, filigreed stone bridges and carved pillars exhibit Persian and Moorish influences, and the use of brilliant blues and golds bring to mind a Mughal palace, but the interior design is modern Indian.

No matter which room is selected, guests wake up to glorious views. All 102 rooms and suites are well-appointed, and include a satellite TV and DVD/CD player. Marble bathrooms add a cool touch, and come equipped with a separate shower and bathtub, along with deluxe toiletries. The Deluxe Rooms with Terraces feature private open-air decks, which are ideal for romantic dinners. The Suites also come with a private terrace and separate living and dining areas.

To bring things up a notch, check into the regal Kohinoor Suite, which offers separate living and dining rooms, as well as a private study and an open-air terrace. In

These days, a trip, whether for business or leisure, is not complete without a spa experience. The Oberoi Spa by Banyan Tree promises treatments originating from the days of Mughal royalty, therapies which have been honed over generations and promise to revive and refresh.

During the 16th and 17th centuries, Agra was the Mughal capital of India. It is no wonder then that many historical sites are found near the hotel. However, it is the Taj Mahal which draws the most attention, and a stay at The Oberoi Amarvilās is among the best ways to experience it.

addition, the luxurious bedroom features a dressing area with a walk-in closet.

To appease appetites, Amarvilās has a number of dining choices available. Its main restaurant is Bellevue, where a fusion of Asian and Mediterranean food is served. In the more formal Esphahan, open only for dinner, traditional Indian food is served. To ensure a truly cultural experience, 'live' performances of the traditional *sitar* and *tabla* take place every evening.

PHOTOGRAPHS COURTESY OF THE OBEROI AMARVILĀS, AGRA.

FACTS		
ROOMS	38 Deluxe Rooms • 57 Deluxe Rooms with Terraces • 4 Executive Suites • 2 Luxury Suites • 1 Kohinoor Suite	
FOOD	Bellevue: Asian-Mediterranean • Esphahan: Indian • Lobby Lounge: snacks	
DRINK	bar	
FEATURES	The Oberoi Spa by Banyan Tree • pool • gym	
BUSINESS	wireless Internet access • meeting rooms • business centre	
NEARBY	Taj Mahal • Fatehpur Sikri • Gwalior • Keoladeo National Park • Agra Fort • Itimad-ud-Daula	
CONTACT	Taj East Gate, Agra 282001, Uttar Pradesh • telephone: +91.562.2231 515 • facsimile: +91.562.2231 516 • email: reservations@oberoi-amarvilas.com • website: www.oberoihotels.com	

The Oberoi, New Delhi

The heritage and architecture of New Delhi are a study in fusion, incorporating elements from the past and present, the East and West. But more than that, they reflect the multi-faceted history of the city, where various religions, cultures and people have lived together in harmony for generations. Visitors are warmly welcomed by a society used to opening its arms to strangers. This warm hospitality is prevalent in The Oberoi, New Delhi, where guests can always expect to find a friendly face and a more than comfortable place to stay.

Located close to the city centre, business travellers in particular will find The Oberoi an ideal place to call home during work trips. Modern, luxurious and well-equipped, with superb service standards, the hotel is the right partner to help seal that deal.

The hotel's range of accommodation options excels in both form and function. Beautifully decked out in contemporary Indian style, the spacious Executive Suite comes with a separate living room which overlooks the well-tended fairways of Delhi Golf Club. The Deluxe Suite comes with a

whirlpool bath, while the Presidential Suite has a special pantry just for the butler. Another option is the exclusive Curzon Suite, which is bigger and grander, and has the best views in the hotel. It is no wonder that this is the suite of choice for dignitaries, VIPs and high-flyers.

Night after night, the hotel's food and beverage outlets are a draw for diners who appreciate the finer things in life. Perhaps the most exciting restaurant is threesixty°, which offers a tantalising menu focusing on three regions currently making a splash in the culinary scene—the Mediterranean, India and Japan. Speciality sections include a sushi station, yakitori grill, wood-fired oven and modern tandoor, all manned by experienced chefs.

Traditional Italian food can be enjoyed at Travertino, which was launched in association with the renowned Hotel Hassler in Rome. Also an option is the award-winning Taipan, where perennial favourites

include the Peking duck and dim sum. Those seeking Indian food must try The Kandahar. Do visit The Gourmet Shoppe too for pastries, chocolates and more delights. After dinner, check out The Club Bar or Enoteca, where an extensive drink menu and a fine selection of Cuban cigars await. Expect all this and more at The Oberoi, New Delhi.

THIS PAGE: Soft lights accentuate the seamless blend of Art Deco pieces with modern design elements in the lobby.

OPPOSITE (FROM TOP): Silk draperies set off the dark wood used in the rooms; the swimming pool is a popular hangout during the day.

PHOTOGRAPHS COURTESY OF THE OBEROI, NEW DELHI.

FACTS

ROOMS	127 Premium Rooms • 122 Deluxe Rooms • 16 Executive Suites • 7 Deluxe Suites • 5 Presidential Suites • 1 Curzon Suite • 1 Duplex Suite
FOOD	Taipan: Chinese • threesixty°: international • The Kandahar: Indian • Travertino: Italian • The Gourmet Shoppe: delicatessen
DRINK	Enoteca Bar and Lounge • The Club Bar
FEATURES	The Oberoi Spa and Fitness Centre by Banyan Tree • pool • beauty salon • chemist
NEARBY	Delhi Golf Club • India Gate • Humayun's Tomb • Jama Masjid • Purana Qila • Rashtrapati Bhavan • Qutb Minar • Red Fort
CONTACT	Dr. Zakir Hussain Marg, New Delhi 110003 • telephone: +91.11.2436 3030 • facsimile: +91.11.2436 0484 • email: reservations@oberoidel.com • website: www.oberoihotels.com

The Park, New Delhi

Dramatic is the word most often used to describe The Park, New Delhi, situated in the city's centre, and overlooking the historic 18th-century Jantar Mantar observatory.

The lobby is styled almost completely in white, with few angular corners and straight lines to disrupt the soothing fluidity...until you arrive at the reception area, that is. Fuchsia accents stand out against the pure white background. This bold use of colour may come as a surprise to those not familiar with The Park's sense of style. The lobby is also an art gallery with permanent and temporary installations by local and foreign artists, making every moment spent there a memorable cultural experience. Guests appreciate the hot pink items on display and have no qualms about sinking comfortably into the deep sofas, while digging their feet into the plush carpet.

The guestrooms and suites are equally eye-catching. The Luxury Rooms are stunning in their simplicity and equipped to suit the needs of all guests. The Residence comprises two floors of lavish rooms and suites which may include a private jacuzzi or sauna, and 24-hour butler service, all designed to pamper. At The Residence Lounge, guests can enjoy breakfast, hold a

business meeting, arrange for a private dinner, or simply unwind during happy hour.

Like its private spaces, The Park's public spaces are equally striking. Fire, the eye-catching contemporary Indian restaurant adjacent to the lobby, is spectacular both by day and night. Smooth steel frames support marble table tops, while numerous tiny lights cast a gentle glow over diners.

Just as impressive is Mist, a restaurant offering all-hours dining, with delectable Italian favourites such as pizza with innovative toppings, pasta and risotto, in addition to Mediterranean and Asian recipes. Mist plays with the element of water through its cool and contemporary design, incorporating a light blue tone with glass and polished steel.

Agni is a bar worth talking about. It is visited every night by the hippest and trendiest party-goers, all eager to enjoy Agni's speciality concoctions and dance the night away. Red and orange predominate, complemented by leather divans and fiery lighting.

Most hotel gift shops tend to have uniformly functional designs. The Box, on the other hand, falls in line with The Park's focus on making an impression. It is accessed via an enticing pink doorway behind the reception's interlocking marble counter tops. Encased in glass, the shop offers unique souvenirs ranging from handicrafts to paintings, beauty products, stationery and accessories. Guests have the widest choice of the finest items to remind them of their stay at The Park, New Delhi.

THIS PAGE: *From heady concoctions to the devilish décor and dance floor, Agni exudes a charm that is impossible to resist.*

OPPOSITE (CLOCKWISE FROM TOP LEFT): *Gentle blue hues, oval lights and a curtain of glass 'droplets' enhance Mist's water theme; colour, space and functionality meet in The Park's guestrooms; the lobby's furnishings, including curved velvet sofas, armchairs and tables with pink light accents, are an art installation unto themselves.*

PHOTOGRAPHS COURTESY OF THE PARK, NEW DELHI.

FACTS		
ROOMS	188 Luxury Rooms • 25 Deluxe Rooms • 7 Deluxe Suites • 4 Presidential Suites	
FOOD	Fire: contemporary Indian • Mist: Italian and Asian • The Park: confectionery • Aqua: international	
DRINK	Agni	
FEATURES	The Spa and Fitness Centre • The Box • The Salon • garden terrace and pool	
BUSINESS	banquet halls • business centre	
NEARBY	Army Golf Club • Jantar Mantar • Connaught Place • Khan Market	
CONTACT	15 Parliament Street, New Delhi 110001 • telephone: +91.11.2374 3000 • facsimile: +91.11.2374 4000 • email: tpnd@theparkhotels.com • website: www.theparkhotels.com	

Trident Hilton Gurgaon

Trident Hilton Gurgaon is a five-star deluxe hotel showcasing a blend of Thai architecture and traditional Indian touches. Located in the central business district of Gurgaon, a part of the National Capital Region, Trident Hilton is close to both the international and domestic airports of New Delhi and is well connected by road to Agra and Jaipur.

Designed by reputed architect Lek Bunnag and interior designer Pia Wanglee of Thailand, this 136-room hotel welcomes every visitor with stunning views of a reflection pool, fire torches and beautifully manicured gardens. The lobby is yet another striking feature, with white Greek Thassos marble and an 18-m-high (60-ft-high) golden dome. This gives guests a first impression of height and space, with tall conical brass sconce lights, high-back chairs, towering ceilings and large glass windows. The windows accentuate the width and length of the corridors and overlook expansive gardens with lush greenery. Because of the hotel's minimalist style, there is an uncluttered, relaxed feel about the place, making it perfect for busy executives and those seeking repose.

The elegantly decorated guestrooms are upholstered in warm earthy shades with intricate silver threadwork on the bed's headboard. The rooms and suites offer views overlooking either the reflection pools, where the water touches the window sill, or the gardens. The Deluxe Rooms come with bathrooms featuring a separate bathtub and shower, and a spacious walk-in wardrobe. Guest services include round-the-clock butler service, high-speed wireless Internet access and an air-conditioning system which allows optimum cooling and heating through

THIS PAGE: The low-rise hotel is distinctly Indian in design, with its smooth domes, clean lines, serene pools and soothing colours.
OPPOSITE (FROM LEFT): Sleek, simple furnishings accentuate the hotel's generous spaces; every bedroom is an enticing haven for travellers.

personalised temperature control. The Presidential Suite and the Executive Suites are popular with top management personnel who prefer the option of in-suite spaces, separate from their living areas, for small meetings and discussions.

Trident Hilton's two restaurants are famed for their innovative décor as well as their cuisine. Cilantro, a restaurant offering all-day dining, serves a wide variety of international cuisine, while Saffron, the fine dining restaurant, is lauded for its North Indian

delicacies and regional delights. The Bar offers a wide selection of wines, spirits and cocktails in a sophisticated ambience. Its speciality, however, is its margarita. Light snacks and beverages are offered at The Pool Bar, which is reserved for hotel guests.

Other exclusive facilities include the state-of-the-art fitness centre with Technogym equipment, the Spa by Angsana, featuring Indonesian therapists offering an extensive range of rejuvenating treatments, and an outdoor heated swimming pool.

FACTS

ROOMS	58 Superior Rooms • 28 Premium Rooms • 43 Deluxe Rooms • 7 Suites
FOOD	Cilantro: international • Saffron: North Indian and regional
DRINK	The Bar • The Pool Bar
FEATURES	Spa by Angsana • pool • fitness centre • gift shop • beauty salon
BUSINESS	high-speed wireless Internet access • meeting rooms • business centre
NEARBY	Red Fort • Qutb Minar • Bahai Temple • National Museum • Sultanpur Bird Sanctuary • Chandni Chowk • Humayun's Tomb
CONTACT	New Delhi National Capital Region, 443 Udyog Vihar, Phase V, Gurgaon 122016, Haryana • telephone: +91.124.2450 505 • facsimile: +91.124.2450 606 • email: reservations.gurgaon@trident-hilton.com • website: www.gurgaon.hilton.com

PHOTOGRAPHS COURTESY OF TRIDENT HILTON GURGAON.

Afghanistan

Jammu + Kashmir

Himachal
Pradesh

Punjab

Pakistan

Haryana

Uttaranchal

rajasthan

People's Republic of China

Delhi

Nepal

Sikkim

Bhutan

> Neemrana Fort-Palace
> Bhandari Jewellers, Jaipur
> The Oberoi Rajvilās, Jaipur
> Rambagh Palace, Jaipur
> The Oberoi Vanyavilās, Ranthambhore

Assam

> The Piramal Haveli at Bagar
> Devi Garh Fort Palace
> The Oberoi Udaivilās, Udaipur
> Taj Lake Palace, Udaipur

Rajasthan

Uttar Pradesh

Bihar

Bangladesh

Gujarat

Madhya
Pradesh

Jharkhand

West
Bengal

Chhattisgarh

Orissa

Arabian Sea

Maharashtra

Bay of Bengal

Andhra
Pradesh

Goa

Karnataka

Lakshadweep

Tamil Nadu

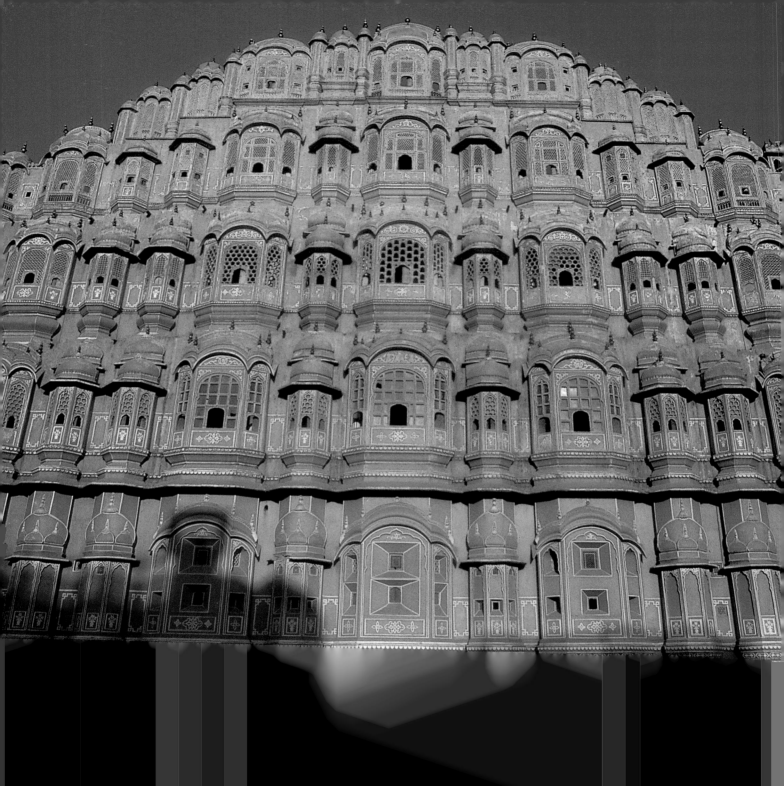

where warrior kings roamed

Visit Rajasthan just once and you will change every preconceived notion you ever had about a desert. Deserts are supposed to be barren, inhospitable, colourless and forbidding, with vultures circling overhead looking for carrion. Nothing could be further from the reality of India's great Thar—or Rajasthani—desert. This 343,000-sq-km (132,436-sq-mile) northwestern state of India with a population of about 44 million is a land of unsurpassed physical beauty, hospitality, romance, legend and colour, and is home to magnificent forts and palaces. Every grain of sand has its own story to tell.

As Colonel James Todd, the celebrated writer once wrote, 'Rajasthan exhibits the sole example in the history of mankind of a people to withstand every outrage barbarity can inflict or human nature sustain, and bent to the Earth, yet rising buoyant from the pressure and making calamity a whetstone to courage.' He was referring to the innumerable wars and battles waged throughout medieval history by Rajasthan's maharajas and princes to protect their region from invaders who lusted after this desert's riches. Rajasthan translates to 'land of the kings', and not without reason. The Rajputs held power here for a thousand years. Rajput means 'son of a prince', and the Rajputs, despite their reputation as relentless and ruthless warriors, adhered to strict codes of honour and chivalry akin to that of the Knights of The Round Table. For every Arthur, Guinevere and Lancelot that Camelot produced, Rajasthan produced twice as many. The Rajputs preferred death over surrender and their kings ruled over expansive lands where they built what are universally acknowledged as the world's most amazing forts and palaces. Rajasthan's history is so lyrical and full of tales that it is told mostly through balladeers who sing of chivalry, romance and the colours that express the state's rugged natural beauty.

During British rule, Rajput rulers hunted with the viceroys and generals, wined and dined them in their palaces at royal balls and special *durbars* (receptions), played polo with them, and romanced their women on palace parapets under the moonlight. They loved spending lavishly on pleasure jaunts to Europe with their families and retinues of

PAGE 94: Rajasthani women crossing the Thar desert.

THIS PAGE (FROM TOP): The state is a land of vast desert plains, but still exudes much beauty; a humble adobe house.

OPPOSITE: Jaipur's Hawa Mahal, or 'Palace of Winds', is Rajasthan's most renowned building.

servants, where entire floors at the fanciest of hotels like The Savoy would be reserved for them. Jaipur's legendary Maharani Gayatri Devi (now in her 80s), described by photographer Cecil Beaton as among the 10 most beautiful women in the world, was often a guest of British royalty, whom she entertained in return in Jaipur. Visitors to the royal palace can view signed photographs of Prince Charles and Diana, Princess of Wales, who stayed there as private guests during their visit to India in 1992. Other photographs of celebrity guests include Jacqueline Kennedy, Queen Elizabeth II and former US president Bill Clinton.

sculpting fantasies

The Rajput kingdoms became part of the Indian republic after 1947. Descendants of these royal families—among them the maharajas of Jodhpur and Jaipur—converted the edifices of their forts and palaces into grand resorts and hotels which have made the state one of the country's major tourist attractions. Some 80 per cent of India's Heritage Hotels are located in Rajasthan. They remind the world that the maharajas, undaunted by the threat of constant attacks from neighbouring states, have left a legacy probably more powerful than their personal bravery in battle, a legacy of creativity in the midst of constant conflict. Cities that are still architectural marvels and masterpieces of town and country planning arose almost mirage-like out of the hot dusty sands. Even with the constant fear of attacks from neighbouring states, the maharajas left their mark on the landscape of the desert. In times of peace, Rajasthani kingdoms exploded with the creativity of craftsmen, painters, weavers, sculptors, poets and musicians who were patronised by the maharajas, to whom cultural pursuits were equal to the pursuit of martial arts and soldiering. Rajasthan's cities, known for their architecture, still overflow with an embarrassment of riches—miniature painting, printed textiles, jewellery, woven products, leather goods and even cuisine.

Folk traditions and music received the patronage of the maharajas and metamorphosed into a popular genre, breeding communities that to this day practice their age-old forms. These traditions were the cradle from which emerged a shopper's paradise. Bundi, Kishangarh, Mewar and Kota have contributed greatly to the art of miniature painting in India.

No one can leave Rajasthan without being part of some festival or celebration. Here is a tongue-in-the-cheek reality check: if there are seven days in a week there are eight festivals in Rajasthan. The Rajasthani loves his ritual and festivity.

The year begins with Sankranti, signifying the end of winter. The people celebrate not just the seasons but also their own land. And the festivities continue in palaces, forts, gaily painted *havelis* (mansions), courtyards, streets and villages, and among the nomads and caravans too. The poets sing and chant, and their mellifluous music mixes with the mood of the desert winds and travels across the sand dunes into every palace, hovel and tent in the region.

The people yearn for harmony. They live in a brutal climate in which they are buffeted by dust storms, starved of adequate rainfall, where night-time temperatures fall rapidly, and where under a merciless summer sun, temperatures can rise up to 52°C (126°F) in the shade. Yet, they reflect not the punishment of the weather but rather the cool and colourful tone of their inner psyche, whose external manifestations are their bright clothes, intricate embroidery and wrist-to-elbow silver jewellery.

live and let live

The common folk fear their gods, work hard, drink hard when they want to, respect their women and treat their guests like gods. Their land, which has a low crime rate, is the safest place to visit in India.

THIS PAGE: *Many of Rajasthan's beautiful palaces and forts have been converted into world-class hotels, such as The Oberoi's Rambagh Palace.*

OPPOSITE (FROM TOP): *Lavishly decorated havelis are a feature of the state; puppets are one of the many items tourists choose to bring home with them.*

The feeling of safety extends to the region's flora and fauna as well. In the desert areas surrounding Jodhpur, the animal-worshipping Bishnoi people have made a religion out of protecting wildlife. In Bishnoi country, the black buck, the shyest of all antelopes and nearly extinct in other parts of north India due to hunting, grazes without fear in the vicinity of herdsmen and their villages. In medieval times, Bishnoi women were so devoted to the desert trees that they would die under the axe-blows of tree fellers who came to chop wood for their landlords and found the women hugging the trees to protect them.

The people of Rajasthan are naturally broad-minded and tolerant. Though they belong to different segments of social and religious groups and speak in several, often mutually incomprehensible, dialects, they respect each other's religious beliefs and sentiments. In this land of sand and scrub, the people have found not conflict but faith. They emit a strange, unfathomable radiance and lust for life. In every home in small villages and the cities they celebrate their innate strength and energy. They express their joy by showing love for and devotion to their deities through song and music and at places of worship. The Rajputs fought mostly Muslim

invaders, and yet, as a testament to their aforementioned broad-mindedness and spirit of tolerance, Hindu, Jain and tribal ritual festivals converge during the Muslim month of mourning. Rajasthan is peppered with places of worship for many of the world's religions. Among the most hallowed—to which Muslim pilgrims throng from all over the world—is the shrine of Sufi saint Khwaja Muin-ud-din Chishti at Ajmer.

the dance of life

Every region of Rajasthan weaves its distinctive lifestyle into music, dance and folk entertainment. Musical instruments vary from single strings stretched across a dried gourd to the sophistication of the *sitar* and the *sarangi*, and from castanets to elaborate drums and rustic violins strummed with the fingers or caressed by a bow and string.

Dances include the *kacchi ghodi* (a dance performed with a dummy horse), fire dance, puppet dance and the gypsy twirls and sensuous movements in which men, women and young children gyrate with glee.

You can be a part of this elaborate song and dance at Rajasthan's fairs, festivals, and processions, including the Elephant Festival, Gangaur, Pushkar, Baneshwar Fair and the Muslim Urs Fair. At every event there are rural bazaars offering exotic trinkets like beads, bangles, old tribal silver jewellery and a comprehensive range of handcrafted items. Most of the bazaars are segmented product-wise, which will make your festival-site shopping a memorable experience.

But a special word is needed about Pushkar. Hindu tradition and scriptures maintain that Lord Brahma—the creator of the world, in a search for his abode on earth, performed the supremely spiritual Vedic Yagna at Pushkar. It is thus the site of the only Brahma temple in the world. It is also the venue for the famous Pushkar Fair, the

THIS PAGE: Pushkar is popular with Hindu pilgrims, who come to bathe in its sacred waters.

OPPOSITE (CLOCKWISE FROM TOP LEFT): Rajasthani women love to adorn themselves with fabrics in bright colours and eye-catching jewellery; an elephant is decorated for a festival; the Pushkar Fair promises scenes you are unlikely to forget.

largest camel and cattle fair in the world, with people coming from all over Asia to buy and sell camels and cattle of international breeds. Fifty-two bathing ghats that are linked to the lunar calendar enclose the lake. Each ghat is believed to have its own miraculous qualities and powers of healing. This city of temples has over 500 of them built over different eras, with varied architectural styles.

ride a magic carpet

A great way to enjoy the mind-boggling diversity of the state, interspersed with shopping, elephant rides, fort tours and gourmet cuisine is to ride the Palace on Wheels, one of the 10 most luxurious trains in the world. During the eight-day trip that takes you through the most haunting destinations of Rajasthan, passengers stay in single or double suites. The 14 air-conditioned coaches which include bars, dining rooms and libraries are luxury personified and decorated like the chambers of the maharajas. A personal valet waits on each guest day and night, serving tea in bed every morning and a nightcap when it is time to sleep. The Palace on Wheels travels by night, stopping during the day to allow passengers to explore various cities under the expert care of English-speaking tour guides.

On this tour, caparisoned elephants and strains of the *shehnai* will welcome you to the 'Pink City' of Jaipur. Lunch at Rambagh Palace and discover Nahargarh Fort, Hawa Mahal and Amber Fort, the silent sentinels of a glorious era. Udaipur is a city of lakes, gardens, palaces, temples and forts. Built around the picturesque Lake Pichola, with the Aravali hills as a backdrop and lovely white buildings skimming the water's edge, Udaipur is one of India's most romantic destinations. It is where you will find the breathtaking Taj Lake Palace, one of the settings for the James Bond film *Octopussy*.

Next, on to verdant Sawai Madhopur and the wild surrounds of Ranthambhore National Park, a Project Tiger reserve. Within this expansive sanctuary lie not only the remains of temples and mosques, but the magnificent 10th-century fort of Ranthambhore. If the 12th-century city of Jaisalmer is not on your itinerary, slot it in,

THIS PAGE (FROM TOP): Intricate latticework gives Rajasthani structures a delicate air; frescoes decorate the interiors and exteriors of many havelis. *OPPOSITE:* The magnificent fort of Jaisalmer has 99 bastions.

for nowhere else will you see a sandstone fort of 99 bastions dominating an entire city. Here, too, are great examples of *haveli* architecture. Both the *havelis* and the homes of poorer folk are equally rich in intricate carvings, latticed windows, seemingly delicate balconies and inviting façades, but to see these forms in all their glory, visit some of the more well-known *havelis* such as Nathmal-ki-Haveli and Patwa-ki-Haveli. Jaisalmer is also where tourists come for the famed camel safaris. These three- or four-day jaunts into the Thar desert can be an utterly romantic affair. Dine under the stars on *bhunwa gosht* (sauteed pieces of spiced tender lamb marinated in yoghurt) and enjoy a cup of *chai* (tea) while the campfire blazes and the camel drivers break into song.

an endless treasure hunt

The markets of Jaipur, Jodhpur, Bikaner and Jaisalmer are a treasure hunter's paradise, a virtual smorgasbord of Indian handicrafts. Textiles, embroidery, jewellery, leather goods, paintings, pottery, puppets and stone or wood products bear the indelible and unique mark of unparalleled artistry associated with Rajasthani craftspeople. Whether you are in a rural area off the beaten track or in a lively urban market, you will find something exclusive to buy.

Of particular interest is Rajasthan's glittering jewellery. Since ancient times, precious and semi-precious stones mined in the state as well as rough-cut gems imported from other parts of India made Rajasthan the jewel in the crown of India's gem trade. Imaginative and highly skilled artisans from Lahore, Delhi, Gujarat and Bengal found their way to Jaipur, Bikaner, Udaipur and Jodhpur and worked on inlay techniques, embedding colourful stones and gems in bracelets, anklets, bangles, arm-bands and even hair combs. Jaipur is the centre for *meenakari* (highly glazed enamel) work and is known for diamond and emerald cutting as well. The Johari and Siredeori bazaars are hotspots for these items. In addition to camel safaris, Jaisalmer is also well-known for its silverwork and antique silver jewellery, which has made its way into many jewel boxes and markets around the world. Pratapgarh in Chittorgarh produces the resplendent *thewa* jewellery, where a thin sheet of gold incorporating a design is fused with molten coloured glass.

Just about every corner of Rajasthan bustles with weavers handcrafting *dhurries* and carpets. The traditional art of tie-dye, known as *bandhani*, which made a huge splash in the early 1960s, is also a Rajasthani tradition. *Laheriyas*—delicate, wavy patterns —are dyed mostly in Udaipur. Other styles include *pachranga,* or five-coloured *bandhej* on saris or turbans. Pottery is India's most ancient art. But the blue pottery of Jaipur—unique as it is the only form of pottery that does not use clay—is one of Rajasthan's most artistic gifts to the world. In Udaipur, shoppers should bear in mind that the city is known for its local crafts, such as miniature painting.

THIS PAGE: Jantar Mantar is one of five observatories built by Maharaja Jai Singh II.

OPPOSITE (FROM TOP): The architectural details on many of Jaipur's buildings are a sight to behold; an ornamented doorway at Amber Fort.

in the pink of health

Rajasthan's capital, Jaipur, popularly known as the 'Pink City', is the logical starting point for anyone travelling in Rajasthan because of its central location and good air, road, and rail connections. The city was founded in 1727 AD by the astronomer Maharaja Jai Singh II. Jantar Mantar, the king's observatory, is a riveting destination. It may look like a giant playground for adults, but in 1734, the year of its completion, it was a supreme example of the achievements of Indian science. It has 18 fixed observational instruments, made of masonry or engraved rings and plates, that measure with pinpoint accuracy the position of the sun, stars and planets. The king built five similar observatories in Delhi, Ujjain and Varanasi; the one in Muttra no longer stands.

Jaipur's pink hue was actually an aesthetic device to create the illusion of red sandstone with which Mughal emperors built their edifices. In 1876, when the Prince of Wales visited Rajasthan, the entire city of Jaipur was painted pink, a colour also associated with hospitality. The best way to explore the city is on foot or by rickshaw. Your sense of adventure should take you into the world of Jaipur's snaking inner lanes where a whole new world, hidden from the tourist in a hurry, waits to reveal its secrets.

Right in the heart of the city, however, is City Palace, a mesmerising display of Rajasthani and Mughal architecture. Huge white and grey marble columns, decorated with floral designs in gold interspersed with coloured stones, are the load-bearing structures for the delicate and perfectly curved arches that have survived the test of time. A section of the compound, known as Chandra Mahal, remains the residence of the royal family, while the rest of the buildings now act as galleries for a superb collection of royal costumes, shawls, armoury, manuscripts and more.

But it is not City Palace that is the architectural icon of Jaipur—rather, it is the Palace of Winds ('Hawa Mahal'). This honeycomb-like construction of pink sandstone was built in 1799 by Maharaja Sawai Pratap Singh as a viewing gallery for the royal ladies. From here one can watch residents go about their daily lives, but these days, locals and tourists gaze at the eye-catching palace from the outside.

One of the most magnificent destinations near Jaipur, situated on the rugged hills outside of town, is Amber Fort, a stunning example of Rajput architecture built in red sandstone and white marble. A real treat for visitors here is the Mirror Palace ('Sheesh Mahal'), found within the Hall of Victory ('Jai Mandir'), which inspires awe with its inlaid panels and multi-mirrored ceiling. Also in Amber is Jaigarh Fort, named after Maharaja Jai Singh II. It dominates a cliff and is surrounded by huge battlements. Inside are secret passageways used by soldiers who lived in barracks, forged their own cannons, prayed in temples located within, and were sustained by a huge granary. From the top of its watchtower, Diwa Burj, visitors enjoy great views and can check out the world's largest wheeled canon, known as Jaya Vana.

To the west lies the desert region of Marwar (Bikaner, Jaisalmer and Jodhpur), and to the north and south the Aravali hills run wild in a jagged fashion. From Jaipur, you can take a leisurely drive to Alwar, the town nearest to the Sariska Tiger Reserve and National Park in the northeast, or to Ajmer, Pushkar and Kishnagarh in the southeast. Also within reach is the Shekawati region in the northwest and popular Ranthambhore National Park in the east.

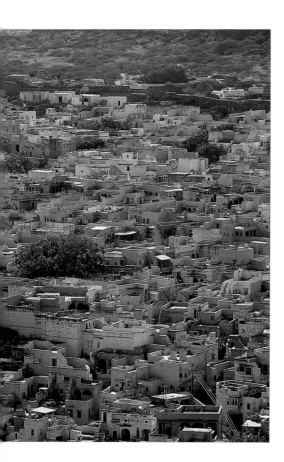

where smiles never vanish

The imperial sun city of Jodhpur was founded in 1459 by Rao Jodha, a chief of the Rathores clan. Known as the 'Blue City'—the town is painted blue to ward off insects—Jodhpur is also famous for a sartorial invention, the simultaneously baggy and tight horse-riding trousers known the world over as jodhpurs.

The magnificent Meherangarh Fort, situated on a 125-m-high (410-ft-high) hill, stands over the city like an immovable guardian angel. The closer you get to it, the more formidable its walls seem. Once through one of its many gates, you will discover a network of courtyards and palaces which now house a museum with a collection of royal memorabilia, including elephant *howdahs* (a seat placed on the elephant) and armoury. Do take a walk to the southern end of the fort for a view across Jodhpur's expanse of cube-like blue buildings.

Beyond the fort, there is much else to explore in the city, including smaller palaces, forts and temples, exquisite handicrafts and schools of folk dances and music. Jodhpur is one of the three larger cities of the Marwar region that also includes Bikaner (once ruled by the family of Maharaja Karni Singh, the great Olympic marksman) and Jaisalmer. Balsamand Lake, an hour's trek from Jodhpur, is a peaceful oasis where you can relax and read a book while shepherds graze their flocks nearby. This is an artificial lake that was built in 1159. Those who cannot get enough of Rajasthan's forts are well advised to check out Khimsar Fort, Rohet Garh, Jhalamand Garh and Luni Fort.

Padharo—every Indian has learned the meaning of this Rajasthani word. It reverberates from the desert, its villages, palaces, traders and artists. It means 'welcome'. Welcome to a land in which a zest for life can be felt all around you, in the smiles that greet you and the colours that surround you. Welcome to a land that reveres guests like divinities and where even enemies are treated with grace. This welcome resonates in the mind of every visitor after he leaves Rajasthan, urging him to return again and again. And return he does, because he wants more of everything he has seen, and wants to see everything he may have missed.

The magnificent Meherangarh Fort...stands over the city like an immovable guardian angel.

Devi Garh Fort Palace

Located in Rajasthan's Aravali hills is the glorious Devi Garh Fort Palace. Lovingly restored, this heritage property dating back to the 18th century is an elegant reflection of a magnificent past.

Bordered by lush foliage and high mountains on three sides, Devi Garh is an all-suite property designed for luxury and indulgence. Each of its 30 suites is uniquely styled and embellished with marble and semi-precious stones.

The exclusive Devi Garh Complex comprises the premium Devi Garh Suite and one of the Palace Suites. A favourite with VIPs, guests who select these rooms have exclusive use of a private black marble swimming pool. The Devi Garh Suite also comes with a private sun deck and jacuzzi.

The spectacular views of the Aravali hills are best seen from the large bay windows or balconies of the Aravali Suite; the most spacious of which is the duplex suite. The décor, from paintings to floor patterns and even the marble courtyard, is centred on the *kamal*, or lotus, considered by many to be the most beautiful symbol in Indian art.

The resplendent colours of Rajasthan are used liberally in the Palace Suites, while the vivid hues of the garden form the design basis of the Garden Suites. Unique to these

THIS PAGE (CLOCKWISE FROM TOP):
Generous proportions and lavish furnishings characterise the décor; rich hues from framed paintings add vibrancy to the suite's solid colours; guests enjoy al fresco dining and great views.

OPPOSITE (FROM TOP): Devi Garh rises majestically from the Aravali hills; local marble was used extensively in the restoration of the 18th-century property.

suites is the traditional *aangan* (courtyard) leading to each Palace Suite, and the private garden with a tented terrace which features in every Garden Suite.

More adventurous travellers seeking to experience the traditional lifestyle of the Rajputs may prefer to book one of Devi Garh's tents, which are erected from October to March. Set up at the foot of the property, the tents recreate the desert sky on cloth ceilings, with shimmering mirrors forming patterns of clouds and stars. Unlike the basic structures of old, however, these tents come replete with modern facilities such as an electric heater, fan, telephone and attached marble-finished bathroom.

Devi Garh's restaurant serves an array of authentic local dishes and international cuisine. A special occasion may call for a customised menu, and may be celebrated at any of the hotel's eight scenic venues, including the rooftop verandah, Silver Lounge, courtyard and garden.

Much like the royalty of the early days, guests are offered time-honoured Ayurvedic therapies and massages for their well-being.

If there is one reason to step outside the magnificent confines of the property, it is to enjoy the charms of Rajasthan. Whether on foot, by bicycle or on organised safaris, the nearby village and temples will surely open your eyes to a very different world.

FACTS

ROOMS	1 Devi Garh Suite • 5 Aravali Suites • 16 Palace Suites • 17 Garden Suites • 8 Deluxe Tents
FOOD	local and international
DRINK	bar
FEATURES	spa • health club • beauty parlour • library • shopping arcade
BUSINESS	Internet access
NEARBY	Delwara village • Eklingji and Nagda temples • trekking • biking • camel safaris • horseback riding
CONTACT	Village Delwara, Tehsil Nathdwara, District Rajsamand, Udaipur 313001, Rajasthan • telephone: +91.2953.289 211 • facsimile: +91.2953.289 357 • email: devigarh@deviresorts.com • website: www.deviresorts.com

Neemrana Fort-Palace

The name 'Neemrana' is derived from a courageous local chieftain who, when defeated in battle, asked that his name be given to his lost kingdom. Built in 1464, the impressive Neemrana Fort-Palace is one of the oldest heritage hotels in India. Located on a magnificent plateau, it is hidden in the horseshoe-like formation of the timeless Aravali hills.

Carved into the hillside, the 10-storey Neemrana Fort-Palace is an awe-inspiring sight, and offers equally stunning views of its surrounds. Visitors have been known to gasp at the sheer splendour of the huge property, both in the day when its grandeur is clearly visible, and at night, when thousands of lights illuminate the hotel, encompassing it in a magical glow.

The stepped property is sprawled over more than 10 hectares (25 acres) across the hills. Extensive restoration works carried out since 1986 have pushed Neemrana Fort-Palace into the ranks of the luxurious heritage properties of the world, with modern conveniences unobtrusively included during the sensitive renovation.

When it comes to accommodation, instead of rooms, there are 48 *mahals*, or palace pavilions; named as such because most of the living spaces are large, exclusive and unique, and were constructed from the existing fort layout. No two *mahals* are the

THIS PAGE: The glorious 15th-century property is carved into the hillside.

OPPOSITE (FROM TOP): Every palace pavilion evokes the feel of a bygone era; soak in the sun and enjoy the magnificent vista from the pool.

by skilled artisans who applied ancient techniques to the stone structure, this wing blends seamlessly with the old fort-palace.

There are many activities to help pass the time here: a game of cards, chess or carrom perhaps, or get into a book from the extensive library. A guided tour of the enormous fort is always a good option, as are excursions to the many historical and cultural sites dotting the area. A favourite with guests are the camel cart rides to the 18th-century stairwell, which descends seven floors below the ground.

same as each has a distinct character, showcased in the décor and the *mahal's* individual stories. Antiques and Rajasthani textiles of various colours and textures are used in the residences. While one suite may boast an original mirrored mosaic ceiling, another may feature ornately carved screen doors or antique lamps. Four-poster beds, plastered walls with *objets d'art* or Indian miniatures, polished mosaic or stone floors and colourful touches add to the character of each comfortable abode. Guests will surely feel like royalty here.

A new wing at Neemrana Fort-Palace comprises a swimming pool with a dramatic view of the village and distant mountains, an Ayurvedic health spa, a conference centre and an open-air amphitheatre. Built

FACTS		
ROOMS	48 *mahals*	
FOOD	local and international	
DRINK	The Lounge	
FEATURES	pool • jacuzzi • library • indoor games • Ayurvedic health centre • yoga classes • guided tours	
BUSINESS	conference rooms • banquet halls • ballroom	
NEARBY	Sariska Tiger Reserve and National Park • camel cart rides • excursions • trekking	
CONTACT	Village Neemrana, District Alwar 301705, Rajasthan • telephone: +91.494.246 006 • facsimile: +91.494.246 005 • email: sales@neemranahotels.com • website: www.neemranahotels.com	

PHOTOGRAPHS COURTESY OF NEEMRANA FORT-PALACE.

The Oberoi Rajvilās, Jaipur

The 'Pink City' of Jaipur holds many surprises for visitors, but few can match The Oberoi Rajvilās, Jaipur, located amidst 13 hectares (32 acres) of well-manicured gardens and shimmering pools.

From a high vantage point, guests who scan the wide expanse of the property may well believe they have found a holiday paradise. Generous outdoor spaces, stately colonnades, domed arches with carved pillars, picturesque bridges and fountains, tasselled garden pavilions and majestically tall trees with wide, overhanging branches all add to the holiday feel.

With grounds fit for royalty, it is no surprise that the interior of the hotel reflects a similar grandeur. Hand-painted frescoes, exquisite chandeliers, the contrast of rich gold and dark wood, and the beautiful symmetry of the many arches radiate a regal air without overwhelming the senses.

Guests can choose from a selection of rooms, villas and tents to spend their nights in, and every one of these is extravagantly appointed with modern conveniences. The rooms and villas come with a thoroughly inviting four-poster bed, and a sunken marble bath overlooking a walled garden.

THIS PAGE: The manicured gardens, distinctive architecture and ornate pavilions recreate the age of the Rajputs.

OPPOSITE: The combination of colourful frescoes, handcrafted brass door frames and an exquisite chandelier result in a lobby which is both breathtakingly beautiful and welcoming.

For a slightly different hotel experience, stay in one of Rajvilās' 14 Luxury Tents. These air-conditioned tents feature teak floors and free-standing bathtubs, with an ambience that is decidedly warm and romantic. An outstanding feature of tent living is the liberal display of skilful embroidery—on the inside of the canopy, cushions and upholstery, pillowcases and bedspreads.

Guests travelling with families will prefer the hotel's Royal Villa. This two-bedroom villa has a private dining room and swimming pool. Its interior is an exercise in simplicity and attention to detail, showcasing modern and traditional Indian craftsmanship.

Though guests may choose to make the most of their rooms with private dining, a trip to the hotel's Surya Mahal restaurant should not be missed. The menu here covers the best of international and Indian cuisine along with a selection of fine wines. Guests may also choose to dine outdoors in the restaurant's courtyard. During the peak season, diners will be entertained by traditional Indian music and dance performances, just like Rajput royalty.

Not only is Rajvilās ideal for a honeymoon or family vacation, it also caters to guests with tasks to complete and work to do. With two fully-equipped conference rooms and dedicated secretarial services, the hotel can host corporate events for up to 35 people in each venue.

No stay at Rajvilās is complete without a visit to The Oberoi Spa by Banyan Tree. Housed in a restored Rajasthani mansion, the spa includes a number of spa suites, treatment rooms and a beauty salon. A menu of holistic treatments from the East and West awaits guests. The spa overlooks the main pool, a focal point of the property.

With so much beauty within the grounds of The Oberoi Rajvilās and so much to savour, from the appetising cuisine to the enticing rooms, guests may find themselves reluctant to leave.

PHOTOGRAPHS COURTESY OF THE OBEROI RAJVILĀS, JAIPUR.

FACTS		
ROOMS	54 Deluxe Rooms • 14 Luxury Tents • 2 Villas • 1 Royal Villa	
FOOD	Surya Mahal: international and Indian	
DRINK	Rajwada Library and Bar	
FEATURES	The Oberoi Spa by Banyan Tree • pool • gym • tennis courts • library • 5-hole pitch and putt	
BUSINESS	boardroom • secretarial services	
NEARBY	Jaipur city • City Palace • Amber Fort • Hawa Mahal • Jaigarh Fort • Nahargarh Fort • Jantar Mantar • elephant safaris • horseback riding	
CONTACT	Goner Road, Jaipur 303012, Rajasthan • telephone: +91.141.2680 101 • facsimile: +91.141.2680 202 • email: reservations@oberoi-rajvilas.com • website: www.oberoihotels.com	

The Oberoi Udaivilās, Udaipur

Situated on the banks of the placid Lake Pichola, The Oberoi Udaivilās awes with its lavish arches, 450 hand-carved columns, gold leaf domes and landscaped terraces. Guests reach the hotel by embarking on a pleasant boat ride across the lake, which accentuates the visual impact of the property. The sight of the hotel will elicit an involuntary gasp as guests take in its grand façade and breathtaking beauty.

Spread generously over more than 12 hectares (30 acres) and bordered on all

sides by a moat, guests almost instantly feel that they have entered another world.

Ten years in the making, this resort hotel is the result of careful consultation between design and building specialists, historians and architects to recreate the likeness of a Rajasthani Mewari palace.

The Rajput inspiration is apparent throughout the hotel and its rooms. Intricate designs, hand-painted murals and artefacts adorn each room. In the courtyard of a Deluxe Room, guests can relax undisturbed under a silk parasol and marvel at the 17th-century palaces on the far side of the lake. Of the 19 Superior Deluxe Rooms, nine have views of the conservatory, while the remaining rooms enjoy lake views.

Without a doubt, the suites are fit for royalty. Already extravagant in size and

THIS PAGE (FROM TOP): Pillows and cushions in vibrant hues add a pleasing touch to the rooms; the Spa Pool, with its serene atmosphere, is ideal for quiet repose or meditation.
OPPOSITE: Each well-appointed Superior Deluxe Room opens onto a walled courtyard and a semi-private swimming pool.

furnishings, guests also enjoy the services of a private butler. The exclusive 246-sq-m (2,650-sq-ft) Kohinoor Suite is ideal for those seeking the best facilities in one place. Included here are a private pool, a courtyard with fountains, fireplaces and a master suite with a wooden sauna and marble-finished bathtub.

Dining at The Oberoi Udaivilās is a joy. Like all things here, the cuisine is superb, the dishes exquisitely presented, and the drinks enticing. Outdoor dining is especially magical, complemented by moonlight, stars, scented candles and soft music.

Situated in a miniature domed palace is The Oberoi Spa by Banyan Tree. Here, guests can choose from numerous non-clinical therapies and emerge totally rejuvenated. Fitness facilities are available at the hotel's two swimming pools and gym.

Outside, in Udaipur, with its age-old palaces, temples and forts, the history and culture of a different era await.

PHOTOGRAPHS COURTESY OF THE OBEROI UDAIVILĀS, UDAIPUR.

FACTS		
ROOMS	63 Deluxe Rooms • 19 Superior Deluxe Rooms • 4 Luxury Suites • 1 Kohinoor Suite	
FOOD	Suryamahal: Western, Asian and contemporary • Udaimahal: Indian and international	
DRINK	bar	
FEATURES	The Oberoi Spa by Banyan Tree • pool • gym	
BUSINESS	conference rooms • secretarial services	
NEARBY	Udaipur city • palaces • forts • temples • gardens	
CONTACT	Haridasji Ki Magri, Udaipur 313001, Rajasthan • telephone: +91.294.2433 300 • facsimile: +91.294.2433 200 • email: reservations@oberoi-udaivilas.com • website: www.oberoihotels.com	

The Oberoi Vanyavilās, Ranthambhore

THIS PAGE: This unique resort is surrounded by an abundance of nature, including fruit trees and a wildlife sanctuary.

OPPOSITE: The luxury tents feature the finest linens and drapes, with motifs suitably inspired by the wild.

Tucked between the Aravali and Vindhya mountain ranges of Rajasthan is an unexpected expanse of luxury. A well-known secret among romantics and adventurers, The Oberoi Vanyavilās, Ranthambhore, is a 'campsite' with a difference.

This resort is located within 8 hectares (20 acres) of landscaped grounds and, despite its rugged surroundings, has all the amenities and conveniences expected by a seasoned traveller. Accommodation takes the form of luxury tents set amidst fragrant lemon and mango trees, located by the banks of a lake filled with carp.

Because the resort borders the world-renowned Ranthambhore National Park and Tiger Reserve, there is the constant thrill of being in proximity of magnificent wildlife, including tigers and leopards. Guests at the resort are frequent visitors to the reserve.

The interior of The Oberoi Vanyavilās is a resplendent display of intricate details and skilled craftsmanship, with furnishings fit for a royal residence. It should be no surprise that

...the log fire crackling in the Inner Courtyard enhances the sense of outdoor adventure.

wildlife is the predominant theme: elephant-embroidered cushions, pictures of exotic birds soaring high in the sky and rugs with animal prints are the norm here.

Each of the 25 tents is designed for luxury. After a hectic day at the wildlife reserve, guests can retreat to a private 72-sq-m (790-sq-ft) sanctuary. A soak in the free-standing bathtub is guaranteed to revive any tired body, as is a nap in the four-poster bed. Polished wooden floors, wall hangings and delicate embroidery on the canopy add a warm touch. Each tent is also conveniently equipped with a television and DVD player, along with an IDD telephone.

Greet the morning sun with a juice in hand from a private deck or garden. A hearty breakfast then awaits at the Dining Room or Inner Courtyard, where guests can feast on the freshest salads and produce from the resort's own gardens.

During the day, intrepid explorers can opt for guided safaris or trek through the remnants of a 1,000-year-old fort. Back at the resort, indulge in a round or two of spa therapy at The Oberoi Spa by Banyan Tree, which offers an extensive menu of treatments to leave you feeling refreshed. Guests can also unwind with a slow swim.

When night falls, the log fire crackling in the Inner Courtyard enhances the sense of outdoor adventure. Once in a while, guests may even discern the calls of the wild, making The Oberoi Vanyavilās the right choice for adventurous romantics.

FACTS		
	ROOMS	25 tents
	FOOD	Dining Room and Inner Courtyard: Western, Asian and Indian
	DRINK	Library Bar
	FEATURES	The Oberoi Spa by Banyan Tree • pool • fitness tent
	BUSINESS	meeting room
	NEARBY	Ranthambhore National Park and Tiger Reserve • ancient forts • temples
	CONTACT	Ranthambhore Road, Sawai Madhopur 322001, Rajasthan • telephone: +91.746.2223 999 • facsimile: +91.746.2223 988 • email: reservations@oberoi-vanyavilas.com • website: www.oberoihotels.com

PHOTOGRAPHS COURTESY OF THE OBEROI VANYAVILĀS, RANTHAMBHORE.

The Piramal Haveli at Bagar

Starkly romantic in the day and softly dreamy at night, The Piramal Haveli at Bagar, Shekhavati, is quite possibly one of the most stately *havelis* of Rajasthan.

Shekhavati is located some 250 km (155 miles) from New Delhi, and its principal attractions are the beautifully painted *havelis* of the Marwaris, a trading community which lived in Rajasthan. From the 19th century, large numbers of Marwaris migrated to Kolkata and Mumbai to make their fortunes before returning to build their *havelis*. So outstanding are these picturesque painted properties that they have earned the region the nickname 'open-air art gallery'.

The Piramal Haveli is the former home of Seth Piramal Chaturbhuj Makharia (1892–1958), a trader who made his fortune in commodities such as cotton, textiles, opium and silver.

Stately yet simple, Piramal Haveli is at times referred to as a 'grand dame', and at other times, a 'non-hotel', because it retains all the charms of the home it once was. Built in 1928 in Rajasthani-colonial style, the eight-room property has courtyards surrounded by pillared porticoes and frescoed walls, with columns of distinct colonial architecture.

...few are as spectacular, nor as lovingly restored.

While modern conveniences and amenities have been added, much of Piramal Haveli's traditional décor has been retained. Paintings of gods, motor vehicles and planes decorate the walls, the latter two reflecting the British presence in India.

Guests can be forgiven for thinking they have stepped into someone's residence, albeit from another age, as the rooms and public spaces sport the authentic furnishings of an earlier era. The predominant use of wood, tiles, cane and rattan; the high ceilings, airy verandahs and beautiful arches; and the well-manicured gardens create an idyllic haven and offer an experience not easily forgotten.

A stay at Piramal Haveli is incomplete without dining at the renowned Marwari, famed for its traditional vegetarian menu. The food, cooked over a slow fire, is specially prepared for guests. The hotel also serves sumptuous meals on the nearby sand dunes, with bonfires lighting up the night sky.

Diners have been known to make a booking just for this privilege months in advance.

On the rare occasion that guests tire of discovering the calm Bagar, they may venture beyond the walls of Piramal Haveli to explore other villages and towns with *havelis*—though few are as spectacular, nor as lovingly restored. Further afield are sights such as the Sati Temple of Jhunjhunu and the town of Nawalgarh, which make for a short but pleasant day tour.

THIS PAGE: *The rattan and cane furniture, hand-painted frescoes and luxurious spaces offer guests a glimpse into the life of the Marwaris.*

OPPOSITE (CLOCKWISE FROM TOP RIGHT): *The lounge area looks just like it did when the Piramal family was in residence; the stately Rajasthani-colonial architecture belies the warmth and hospitality within the hotel; enjoy a well-prepared meal outdoors.*

FACTS		
	ROOMS	8 rooms
	FOOD	Marwari: traditional vegetarian
	FEATURES	library • cards • indoor games • carrom • badminton
	NEARBY	Shekhavati town • Sati Temple • Nawalgarh • Jhunjhunu
	CONTACT	Village and PO Bagar 333023, District Jhunjhunu, Shekhavati, Rajasthan • telephone: +91.1592.221 220 • email: sales@neemranahotels.com • website: www.neemranahotels.com

PHOTOGRAPHS COURTESY OF THE PIRAMAL HAVELI AT BAGAR.

Rambagh Palace, Jaipur

The mention of Rajasthan inevitably brings to mind an age of polo-playing princes astride their powerful steeds, royal parties and the regal palaces where they were held. For almost two centuries, Rambagh Palace, Jaipur was home to generations of monarchs, and was witness to their revelry.

In 1957, Rambagh Palace opened its doors as a luxury hotel, offering guests the opportunity to experience the royal lifestyle.

The hotel stands amidst 19 hectares (47 acres) of well-manicured gardens and is an architectural marvel—a flawless blend of Mughal and Rajput designs. Rambagh Palace impresses with its cusped arches, carved pillars, elegant domes and high ceilings which are evocative of grand Indian palaces, with intricate frescoes and period furniture affirming its grandeur.

Rambagh Palace is well known for its upscale facilities and unparalleled service standards. Every room and suite has been carefully refurbished to meet the needs of guests while keeping to the royal theme. Each space is stunning in design, with delicate finishes such as textured wood panels, complicated mirror and stone work, pillars with marble inlay and unique hand-paintings. French windows open to offer views of lush greenery or the courtyard of the generous compound. Some of the suites were the personal chambers of the maharajah of Jaipur and the royal family, which means guests can literally live like

THIS PAGE (FROM TOP): Chandni Chowk, the central courtyard of the hotel, is an idyllic place for quiet strolls; the hotel's architecture is a seamless blend of Mughal and Rajput elements.

OPPOSITE: The Suryavanshi Suite is decorated with unique artefacts and period furniture reflecting Rajasthan's heritage.

royalty and enjoy the magnificent opulence of the décor and furnishings.

The fine-dining restaurant, Suvarna Mahal, which means 'palace of gold', lives up to its name, with its high ceiling, gilded mirrors and Italian frescoes. To the strains of classical music, chefs whip up the best of royal Indian cuisine. At the Rajput Room, guests enjoy an array of cuisines.

Steam, a restaurant-cum-bar on wheels, is styled after a Victorian steam engine and includes a 'train station' where guests can relax in an innovative environment.

Those looking to hold a special event at Rambagh Palace will appreciate the hotel's banquet facilities. Its meeting rooms and an adjacent conference centre can hold up to 80 and 350 guests respectively. And when the sun sets, Rambagh Palace's well-tended gardens can be converted into a huge function area illuminated by twinkling lights—the perfect venue for weddings or outdoor parties of up to 3,000 people.

PHOTOGRAPHS COURTESY OF RAMBAGH PALACE, JAIPUR.

FACTS		
ROOMS	44 Luxury Rooms • 13 Historical Suites • 3 Royal Suites • 2 Grand Royal Suites • 1 Grand Presidential Suite	
FOOD	Suvarna Mahal: Indian • Rajput Room: multi-cuisine	
DRINK	Polo Bar • Steam	
FEATURES	indoor and outdoor pools • fitness centre • spa • yoga and meditation classes • tennis • table tennis • squash • croquet • jogging track • polo • putting green	
BUSINESS	Internet access • conference rooms • secretarial service	
NEARBY	golf • cultural and heritage buildings • ancient forts • bazaars	
CONTACT	Bhawani Singh Road, Jaipur 302005, Rajasthan • telephone: +91.141.2211 919 • facsimile: +91.141.2385 098 • email: rambagh.jaipur@tajhotels.com • website: www.tajhotels.com	

Taj Lake Palace, Udaipur

Rising out of Lake Pichola, Taj Lake Palace, Udaipur evokes a sense of magic and mysticism. Surrounded by the majestic Aravali hills on one side and regal palaces on the other, this white marble hotel is almost dreamlike in appearance.

Dating back some 250 years, Taj Lake Palace holds fast to the proud traditions of Indian royalty while offering the most advanced facilities and services. Like the honoured guests of the maharana of days past, hotel guests enjoy the kind of luxurious living hitherto reserved only for officials of the highest court.

The sensitively restored pavilions, archways, towers and carvings reflect the diverse styles of the property's previous royal residents, each with his unique artistic preferences. However, the nuances in style blend seamlessly to create a distinctly Indian opulence. Scenic courtyards with well-kept lawns, lily-filled ponds and gushing fountains are perennial favourites, and indoor spaces are creatively expansive, filled with period pieces and extravagant embellishments.

All the guestrooms and suites offer spectacular views of the surrounding lake, mountains and palaces. Guests can lie back on a comfortable recliner on the private terrace of a Luxury Room, and lazily survey the scenery while sipping from a glass of chilled Champagne.

The Chandra Prakash Suite has the distinction of being the only room at Taj Lake Palace where the maharana held court in the 1930s. Indian-style chandeliers, gilt mouldings and dainty fretwork screens complement the rich fabrics and dark wood four-poster bed and furnishings, adding to the grandeur of the suite.

Not only do guests live like royalty at Taj Lake Palace, their dining experiences are also stately affairs. Neel Kamal is renowned for its authentic Rajasthani fare, which is wood-fired to perfection. Overlooking the lily pond, this fine dining restaurant boasts interiors inspired by royal banquet halls, with richly hued upholstery, lavish décor, stylish crockery and crystalware.

All-day dining is available by the lake at Jharokha, while after-dinner drinks can be enjoyed at the Amrit Sagar bar. The bar is known for its extensive selection of vintage wines and spirits.

Executives looking for a one-of-a-kind venue for corporate events will appreciate Taj Lake Palace for its unparalleled service and unique facilities. Indoor and outdoor events can be held at the hotel or onboard a ceremonial barge.

Taj Lake Palace also has a number of health and recreational facilities, including the Royal Spa, fitness centre and a shopping arcade. More strenuous activities such as trekking, mountain biking and horseback riding can be easily arranged by the hotel.

THIS PAGE (FROM TOP): The coloured glass windows of the Khush Mahal Suite will definitely make an impression; the picturesque lily pond courtyard is ideal for private functions and romantic moments.
OPPOSITE: The Chandra Prakash Suite is the epitome of old-world charm with its sculpted pillars, hand-painted murals and ornate finishings.

FACTS		
ROOMS	49 Deluxe Lake-Facing Rooms • 17 Luxury Rooms • 1 Royal Spa Suite • 7 Royal Suites • 8 Grand Royal Suites • 1 Grand Presidential Suite	
FOOD	Neel Kamal: Rajasthani and Indian • Jharokha: multi-cuisine	
DRINK	Amrit Sagar	
FEATURES	Royal Spa • Gyan Sagar reading and games room • pool • fitness centre • jacuzzi • ceremonial barge • shopping arcade	
BUSINESS	Internet access • meeting rooms • secretarial services • laptop computers for hire	
NEARBY	ancient forts, temples and palaces • jeep safaris • horseback riding • trekking	
CONTACT	PO Box No. 5, Pichola Lake, Udaipur 313001, Rajasthan • telephone: +91.294.2528 800 • facsimile: +91.294.2528 700 • email: lakepalace.udaipur@tajhotels.com • website: www.tajhotels.com	

PHOTOGRAPHS COURTESY OF TAJ LAKE PALACE, UDAIPUR.

Bhandari Jewellers, Jaipur

THIS PAGE AND OPPOSITE: *Every beautiful accessory at Bhandari Jewellers is skilfully handcrafted and set with stones of unrivalled lustre and quality. Perennial in appeal, the designs bring together the finest traditions of India and the contemporary styles most desired by today's consumers.*

Bhandari Jewellers has amassed an impressive and loyal customer base from both India and overseas. If you are looking for exquisite handcrafted accessories embellished with glittering stones; silver and brass artefacts; and the most exquisite silk and paper paintings, you need not go very far in Jaipur. Bhandari Jewellers has a wonderful selection, and if this is not enough, their in-house experts can customise pieces to suit your needs.

Set in the heart of Jaipur, Bhandari Jewellers has gained a reputation for offering gems unrivalled in quality and excellent craftsmanship. While its contemporaries have remained rooted in traditional designs, Bhandari Jewellers has kept abreast of evolving international tastes and trends. Its exceptional collections boast a seamless and innovative mix of time-honoured designs, with contemporary settings and finishes that will win the heart of any connoisseur of fine jewellery.

A visit to Bhandari Jewellers is almost like a trip to a house of treasures. Customers usually find themselves awestruck by the presentations of shimmering and lustrous enamelled and handcrafted jewellery studded with precious and semi-precious stones such as diamonds, emeralds, pearls and rubies, encased in silver, white and yellow gold; marble-accented ornaments; and exotic figurines. As there is an in-house manufacturing facility, Bhandari Jewellers is able to oversee the quality and workmanship of its products from the start of the production process, to the finish. Living up to its reputation as a forerunner in the industry, the company engages only craftsmen, designers and silversmiths who are trained and well-practised in traditional and modern jewellery-making methods. As the staff proudly declare to every customer who walks through the door, each item is individually and completely handmade, and comes with a certificate of guarantee.

Royalty, dignitaries, international designers and Hollywood celebrities have all visited and bought keepsakes from the store to bring home. Among these luminaries are ex-Beatle Sir Paul McCartney, English cricket star David Gower, tennis ace and Wimbledon champion Boris Becker and the Queen of Sweden. Many others have returned to Bhandari Jewellers for more precious items, sometimes armed with stones and designs of their own. Show the craftsmen the design you want, and they will create an excellent reproduction for you.

An established outfit which has been at the forefront of the industry for more than three decades, Bhandari Jewellers is a must-visit for anyone who appreciates beauty.

PHOTOGRAPHS COURTESY OF BHANDARI JEWELLERS, JAIPUR.

FACTS

PRODUCTS   handcrafted jewellery set with precious and semi-precious stones • enamel jewellery • silver and brass handicrafts • silk and paper paintings • artefacts • sandalwood figurines

FEATURES   certificate of guarantee • in-house manufacturing facilities • customisation services

NEARBY   City Palace • Jantar Mantar • Hawa Mahal • forts

CONTACT   5 Dashera Kothi, Amer Road, Jaipur 302002, Rajasthan • telephone: +91.141.2630 654/2630 658/2632 276 • facsimile: +91.141.2630 632 • email: vipulbhandari@hotmail.com • website: www.bhandarijewellers.com

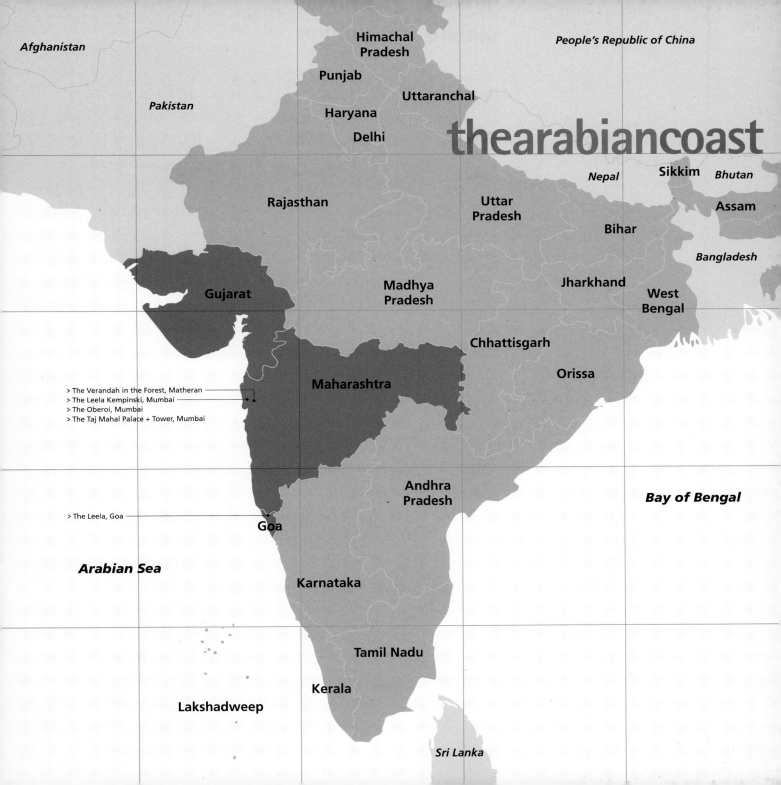

Afghanistan

Pakistan

People's Republic of China

Himachal
Pradesh

Punjab

Uttaranchal

Haryana

Delhi

thearabiancoast

Nepal   Sikkim   Bhutan

Rajasthan

Uttar
Pradesh

Assam

Bihar

Bangladesh

Gujarat

Madhya
Pradesh

Jharkhand

West
Bengal

Chhattisgarh

Orissa

> The Verandah in the Forest, Matheran
> The Leela Kempinski, Mumbai
> The Oberoi, Mumbai
> The Taj Mahal Palace + Tower, Mumbai

Maharashtra

Andhra
Pradesh

Bay of Bengal

> The Leela, Goa

Goa

Arabian Sea

Karnataka

Tamil Nadu

Kerala

Lakshadweep

Sri Lanka

the caress of the arabian sea

Think of India's western coast and visions of sun-kissed beaches, a rich cultural heritage, the birthplace of Mahatma Gandhi, the kingdom of the Hindu god Krishna, Bollywood and dramatic ocean scenes come to mind. In this region lie the states of Maharashtra, Gujarat and Goa, kissed by the Arabian Sea and blessed with the first moisture-laden caresses of the southwest monsoon.

Gujarat, with its 1,600-km (994-mile) coastline, the longest of the Indian states, is an important stop for Hindu pilgrims, who make their way to the remote town of Dwarka to honour Lord Krishna. Dwarka is one of the four most holy Hindu sites in India. According to legend, Lord Krishna set up his capital here after fleeing Mathura some 3,500 years ago.

Along the same coast lies the state of Maharashtra, India's third-largest state, with the 720-km-long (447-mile-long) Konkan coastline bordered by the spectacular Western Ghats. The Ghats, stepped mountains in this instance, are among India's greatest miracles of biodiversity. A unique feature of India is that with only two per cent of the earth's landmass, it boasts a natural wealth far in excess of its actual size. The Western Ghats contribute in no small way to this phenomenon. Of the total higher plant species recorded in India, about 27 per cent are from this region.

As for Goa, the word 'paradise' sums up beautifully the draw of this former Portuguese enclave. It has a slightly different feel from the rest of the country. Here, Roman Catholicism is a major religion, the architecture is different due to the influence of the Portuguese, and there is a laid-back beach vibe that permeates the town.

the muscle of mumbai

Mumbai is the financial nerve centre of India and the capital of Maharashtra. This great metropolis has been described as India's Shanghai, Manhattan, Hong Kong or Singapore, and is more famously known as the home of Bollywood, the largest film industry in the world. Officials may tell you that the city shuts down at certain

PAGE 128: *All sorts of sea-going vessels ply the waters of the Arabian Sea.*

THIS PAGE: *For a taste of scuba diving in India, pay a visit to Goa.*

OPPOSITE: *The sun, sand and sea meet along India's western coast in the most pleasing locations.*

THIS PAGE (FROM TOP): *Feast your eyes on ancient paintings in the Ajanta Caves; great Hindu, Buddhist and Jain sculptures can be found at Ellora.*
OPPOSITE: *A bird's eye view of the city, with its mix of old and new.*

prescribed hours, but 'Mumbaikars' wink at this because the city never sleeps and there are traffic jams at 3 am, when roadside eateries and beach dives are doing a roaring business. Its more than eight million residents are in perpetual motion.

As the world's largest textile market, a major industrial centre and the country's busiest port, Mumbai handles over 40 per cent of India's maritime trade and contributes around 50 per cent to the national exchequer.

It is a city of mind-boggling contrasts. Pavement-dwellers and slums co-exist with modern skyscrapers and graceful colonial columns. The smoke-darkened remains of textile mills stand cheek-by-jowl with shining, newly constructed mills. The steeples of Catholic churches, spires of Hindu temples and minarets of Muslim mosques indicate the existence of an eclectic social and religious culture. But against these finely balanced contradictions stands the indelible face of ancient India, whose Hindu and Buddhist rock-cut caves lie scattered across the land.

heritage at your doorstep

Barely 11 km (6.8 miles) away on the island of Elephanta are caves dating back to the 6th century, with columns and caverns hewn and sculpted from hard rock. Its highlights are the iconic three-headed Shiva sculpture, depicted in large panels. Further away, about 400 km (249 miles) east of Mumbai, near Aurangabad city, are Ellora and Ajanta, the former a series of religious structures in caves, and the latter Buddhist caves featuring well-preserved paintings. Ellora's distinguishing feature is that its structures were carved by generations of monks, both Hindu, Buddhist and Jain, which means the caves have monasteries, chapels and temples within them, the most famous of which is Kailasa Temple, the world's largest monolith. The 30 Ajanta Caves were carved into the face of a horseshoe-shaped gorge along the Waghore River, and house *chaityas* (sacred places and/or items) and *viharas* (temple halls).

Within the city of Mumbai itself, however, there are a number of glorious edifices, though from a modern age—the era of the British Raj. The towering reminder of this

legacy is the Gateway of India, a favourite tourist haunt. It is a rare specimen featuring a combination of European pomp and Indian artistry—a perfect architectural hybrid erected to commemorate the royal visit of King George V and Queen Mary in 1911. The entire structure was only completed, however, in 1924. If it marks the height of the Raj, it also symbolises the setting of the sun on the Indian empire; after independence in 1947, Britain's last soldiers in India marched out through this same gate.

Mumbai's Victoria Terminus is not just one of the world's busiest railroad junctions and the point from which the city's first train chugged out. It is also considered one of the world's most spectacular Gothic buildings. From afar it resembles a mighty cathedral with its domes and stained glass windows displaying engravings and carvings of lions, peacocks, monkeys, gargoyles and elephants. In sharp contrast, some distance away are the lofty minarets of the Haji Ali Mosque, reaching out to embrace the skies. The mosque is built on a platform on the sea. In this city, too, are the only existing Zoroastrian fire temples built by Mumbai's Parsis, whose ancestors fled to India in the 8th century to escape religious persecution.

when in rome...

When you visit Mumbai, it does not take long to become a Mumbaikar yourself and get drawn into the city. Unlike many Indian hubs, tourists are never brazenly stared at in Mumbai. People mind their own business and taxis rarely cheat on fares. And though it is not free of crime, it is one of the safest cities in India for locals and tourists.

When you are here, do as the Mumbaikars do: coast down Marine Drive, the city's favourite waterfront promenade with its beach, mini recreational parks, pony rides and hundreds of vendors selling coconut milk, local delicacies and ice cream. Watch the sun set over the Arabian Sea, and as night falls, find out for yourself why Marine Drive is referred to as 'the Queen's necklace'. At Chowpatty Beach, forget about swimming, instead, find a *malish*-wallah (masseur) and get a head massage.

Walk through the Hanging Gardens, laid out in 1881 on top of a reservoir on Malabar Hills, and then head over to another great attraction, Kamala Nehru Park, which adjoins the gardens. This is an absolute must-visit for kids as there is a giant 'Old Woman's Shoe' where even adults can play hide-and-seek. The park is the best place to feast your eyes on a panoramic view of the city and Marine Drive.

Browse to your heart's content in the Indo-Saracenic style Prince of Wales Museum, with its enviable collection of terracotta figurines from the Indus Valley, old firearms, ivory carvings, statues, a large collection of miniatures and even a portrait of the 16th president of the US, Abraham Lincoln.

You are bound to find something to do in Mumbai that suits your taste, be it cultural performances, heritage tours, walks in the park or shopping. And yes, there is much to shop for in Mumbai. At Colaba Causeway, find yourself overwhelmed by rows of hawkers' stalls and shops selling garments such as original sportswear.

THIS PAGE: *Churchgate Train Station is another great colonial edifice in Mumbai.*

OPPOSITE (FROM LEFT): *The abundance of posters alert visitors to the fact that they are in Mumbai, India's metropolis; as with most of India, religions meet and co-exist in Mumbai.*

For antiques and other interesting items, try Merewether Road, just behind the grand Taj Mahal Palace and Tower. There are a number of shops here selling quality items, but these tend to be pricier. Alternatively, head to Mumbai's bazaars and markets such as Chor Bazaar and Mini Market. Another popular spot is Crawford Market, where the top items are fruit and vegetables. Tourists head here to check out bas reliefs by Lockwood Kipling—father of author Rudyard Kipling—which embellish the exterior of the structure.

the party's never over

Eating out and partying are part of Mumbai's inimitable lifestyle, and there's just about every type of food and cocktail at almost every block, from exclusive haunts at the top hotels to old fashioned Iranian cafés unrivalled by any other Indian city. One of Mumbai's specialities, though not many restaurants serve it, is Bombay Duck—dried fish served crisp from a hot griddle.

THIS PAGE: *The Gateway of India is a stunning structure that will surely catch your eye.*
OPPOSITE (BELOW): *Crowds gather at Mumbai's fascinating markets to buy everything under the sun.*

Among countless excellent pubs and bars, some stand out. Geoffrey's could be a pub straight out of London. The atmosphere is laid-back and the soft music played is mostly from the 1970s and 1980s. It is a great place for lunch as well, especially if you are into soups, sandwiches and carved meat. Jolly Rogers is another popular hangout for Mumbai's yuppies, models and designers from the fashion industry. This pub is built of wood in the shape of a pirate ship, and the waiters and busboys wear typical pirate outfits, carry rapiers and don eyepatches. One spot that is known for its clientele of travellers is Leopold Café and Bar. This pub, dating back to 1871, is a Mumbai institution, and has a wide menu which includes Indian and Western dishes.

Mumbai's 372-sq-m (4,000-sq-ft) Fire and Ice is the city's most happening nightclub. Its gracefully designed interiors have a chrome and steel finish that goes very well with the rock music, heavy metal and New Age music that is played. It has a friendly atmosphere where singles mingle and Mumbai's most beautiful women hang out with their friends while dressed in designer clothes from all over the world.

land of the marathas and the mahatma

The other great city of Maharashtra is nearby Pune, where the Indian Film and Television Institute and the Max Mueller Centre for German Studies are situated. Historically, Pune was the pride and joy of the land of the Maratha-speaking people. The state's heroes lived, fought and died here, among them Shivaji, the revered Maratha king who took on the might of the Mughal Empire under Emperor Aurangzeb. Some of Mumbai's wine-and-dine culture is now infecting Pune as well. One place to check out is Farshid's, which serves Indian and Continental food. French, Italian, Tandoori and coastal Mangalorean cuisines co-exist happily on the menu. Another Pune must-try is Arthur's Theme in Koregaon Park. The restaurant has a stylish look and serves French and European delights.

The Western state of Gujarat, north of Maharashtra, is often described as the 'Manchester of the East', because of the industrial city of Ahmedabad. The state's capital Gandhinagar was named after Mahatma Gandhi, the nation's founding father.

But the main attraction for the visitor to Gujarat is the Gir Forest where the only surviving Asiatic lions roam free. To see these endangered lions, head to the Sasan Gir Wildlife Sanctuary. Also a Gujarat highlight is the Temple of Somnath, where you will find one of the 12 most sacred Shiva shrines in India. Travellers who appreciate ancient history must pay a visit to Lothal, the 4,500-year-old site of a Harappan or Indus Valley civilisation that traded with ancient Egypt, Mesopotamia and Persia.

here we come, goa!

To the south of Gujarat and Maharashtra lies Goa. Its coastline is puny—just 107 km (67 miles)—compared with its two other western sister states, but it compresses within its 3,702-sq-km (1,429-sq-mile) fold just about everything that humankind finds exotic, noble, rare, exhilarating, edifying and, yes, mouth-watering and finger-licking good. Goa is the smallest state in India with a population of about 1.5 million, but it is the most popular with tourists. During the peak season, the number of tourists in Goa just

about equals the number of its local population. In fact, Goa accounts for about 12 per cent of all foreign visitors arriving in India every year.

Those who visit this sun-kissed state for the first time, including Indians, remark that it does not look like an Indian city, and that it looks more like something out of Europe or the Mediterranean. Panaji, Goa's capital is like Portugal in miniature—narrow cobbled streets with houses on both sides, balconies jutting out and filled with flowering creepers and dangling potted shrubs, terracotta-tiled roofs, freshly painted neighbourhood churches, and family-run bars and cafés.

Many liken it to Rio de Janeiro because of its carnivals and cathedrals. But get to know Goa and its history, and you will discover the same themes as you do in every part of India—the ancient, colonial, multi-lingual, multi-religious and the modern all merge to create one colourful whole. You will discover that Goa's history dates back to the 3rd century BC, when it belonged to the great Maurya Empire. At least four other dynasties ruled it until 1312 when Goa fell into the hands of the Muslims, whose reign lasted almost 200 years. Then came the Portuguese (and the missionaries) in 1510, having been unable to secure a base on the Malabar coast further south due to opposition from the Zamorin of Calicut and the Turks, who controlled the trade routes across the Indian Ocean.

good things come in small packages

Goa attracts people from all over the world because it is laid-back, lively and modern, with simple but luxurious accommodation options, sparkling beaches where you can swim and snorkel or simply soak up the sun while sipping the local alcoholic brew *feni*—made from distilled cashew apple juice. Because it is small, Goa can be explored intimately even on a short visit. But you will definitely end up wanting to spend more time here. A visit to Goa is like a modern treasure hunt as there is so much to discover. One of India's best maintained network of roads connects the main town with villages further away, and getting there is just part of the fun. You can ride pillion

THIS PAGE (FROM TOP): *Classic Goan dishes will whet your appetite for more; Goan house architecture reflects the influence of the Portuguese.*

OPPOSITE (FROM TOP): *The endangered Asiatic lion calls Gujarat home; unwind on a tranquil beach in Goa.*

on speeding motorcycle taxis—an experience worth remembering even if it is hair-raising, hop on a flat-bottomed ferry or homemade catamaran which will transport you over water, or just ferry your vehicle across rivers from one stop to the next.

Choose from top hotels with plenty of facilities, or affordable, comfortable and clean cottages right on the beach, which offer simplicity and tranquillity.

sights, sounds and scents

So why else is Goa unique? For one thing, its Latin architecture sets it apart from any other Indian state. Furthermore, the local eating habits are different. Goans love their seafood—fish, shrimp, squid and crabs—and when it comes to meat, they are more inclined to pork or fiery hot sausages. Also, alcohol is more easily available at low prices, and public drinking is more socially acceptable than in other parts of India.

And then there are the beaches. Actually, Goa's virgin beaches were one of the best-kept Indian secrets until the mid-1960s, when they were discovered by American and European hippies. These long-haired flower-children found the living cheap, the booze inexpensive, the sun kind and compassionate, and the local tolerance levels high when it came to nudity and recreational drug use. That is definitely not the case now. Goan authorities are still tolerant but nude sunbathing and the use of drugs can land you in deep trouble with the authorities.

Visitors are spoilt for choice when it comes to the beaches. There are over 40 at your disposal, and the best time to visit is from late October to early May, before the monsoon sets in. If you like bustling crowds, sun loungers, revellers, music and dancing, some good choices are Calangute, Baga and Anjuna. If your preference is serenity, reading quietly and meditating, then your best bets are Colva, Benaulim and Agonda. Anjuna, which is 18 km (11.2 miles) from Panaji, has a double attraction: it has a busy and boisterous flea market that first-time visitors never forget. You can bargain for

knick-knacks, costume jewellery, bracelets and papier-mâché boxes, and snack on seafood delicacies while you shop. The beaches where you will find Goa's more upmarket resorts are Candolim, Sinquerim, Varca and Cavelossim.

the gothic and the baroque

For morning sightseeing, visit the slopes of Altinho Hill. It is unlikely that you will ever forget the view of Panaji and the Mandovi River from this location. Later, head for Dona Paula to take in the majesty of India's largest natural harbour, Mormugao. A trip to Old Goa, 10 km (6.2 miles) east of Panaji, is a must. Old Goa is Christian Goa. The churches in this area were built in the 16th and 17th centuries in the Baroque Renaissance style with some Gothic influences.

THIS PAGE: Check out Goa's beachside flea markets for unique mementos.

OPPOSITE (FROM TOP): Portuguese influence is probably most apparent in Goa's churches; the accommodation options are endless.

The largest church in the entire state is the mid-16th century Se Cathedral. Its 'Golden Bell' rings thrice daily—a wondrous, medieval sound that is heard throughout Old Goa. Other places of interest include the Church of St Cajetan, which was modelled on St Peter's in Rome, and the Royal Chapel of St Anthony.

The most holy place in this area is perhaps the Basilica of Bom Jesus, which houses the three-tiered marble tomb of St Francis Xavier. His remains are preserved in an air-tight silver-and-glass casket. St Francis died in 1552 in Sancian, off the coast of China, and was buried there. But in 1554, his body was exhumed and brought to Goa where he had been sent by the Pope to preach Christianity in 1541.

The state's Christian heritage is further reflected in the number of feast days and festivals it celebrates. These include the feasts of Three Kings, Our Lady of Miracles, St Anthony, St John and, of course, St Francis Xavier.

simply scrumptious

Because Goa is one of the world's favourite tourist haunts, it has the usual wide ranging choice of traditional and luxurious dining options throughout the state. These range from restaurants in five-star hotels to numerous family-run eateries and beach shacks that offer superb food in both local and Western styles.

But it is Goa's Portuguese-influenced cuisine that must be experienced as it is truly a sensation for the tastebuds. *Chourisso*, Goan sausage, and *sorpotel*, stew made with pig liver, kidneys and heart, are two tantalisingly popular pork dishes that show the influence of the Portuguese. But the most famous pork dish to come out of Goa is vindaloo—boneless chunks of pork cooked with red chillies, garlic, vinegar and brown sugar, the pièce de résistance on festive occasions. If there is one dish you must try before leaving Goa, this is it. Other popular Portuguese-Goan dishes include *recheiado*, which is fish stuffed with a spicy red sauce, and *xacuti*, a spicy meat dish cooked with coconut milk and flesh. So let Goa and all its charms—culinary, architectural and natural—draw you in, captivate you and leave you wanting more.

THIS PAGE (FROM TOP): *Pork vindaloo is a Goan speciality; the lavishly ornate interior of St Francis Church.*
OPPOSITE: *The Church of Our Lady of the Immaculate Conception is the main church of Panaji.*

...let Goa and all its charms—culinary, architectural and natural—draw you in...

The Leela, Goa

Located along the quiet west coast of India is the seaside town of Goa, known the world over for its beautiful resorts and pristine beaches. One such property, The Leela, Goa, bordered by the River Sal and Mobor beach, also fronts the Arabian Sea.

This secluded beach resort, voted by *Condé Nast Traveler* readers as one of the 10 best luxury resorts in the world, was conceptualised with exclusivity and style as its guiding principles.

Guests with some knowledge of architecture will immediately recognise that The Leela draws its architectural inspiration from the temples and palace designs of south India's Vijayanagara Empire as well as the Portuguese, but the décor is undeniably modern and sophisticated.

Ever the pioneer, The Leela was the first hotel in India to be conferred the prestigious Imperial Mark for best practices. In particular, it was commended for its service standards and professionalism. It joins a select list of recipients including Oracle, Omega of Switzerland, Rolex, and hotels such as The Dorchester of London and The Carlyle in New York.

Set amidst more than 30 hectares (75 acres) of landscaped gardens and clear lagoons are 137 rooms, suites and villas. The Club at The Leela adds 15 one-bedroom suites to the accommodation options.

THIS PAGE (FROM TOP):
Enjoy a leisurely game of golf on well-manicured fairways and greens; the use of vibrant colours makes The Leela, Goa instantly recognisable.
OPPOSITE: Unwind with a cocktail at the lovely Club Pool.

Every guestroom comes with a spacious balcony or patio, ideal for quiet moments with loved ones or for relaxation, with a view across the serene waters of the lagoons. Guests at the Royal Villas and Presidential Suite wake up to glorious ocean views, and have the added benefit of a private plunge pool.

Always a leader in the hospitality trade, The Leela raised the bar for luxury living and fine service when it launched The Club at The Leela, becoming the first hotel in India to introduce the unique concept of having a resort within a resort.

The embodiment of smart living and superb service, The Club is truly a haven for a select few. Among the special privileges guests at The Club can expect are airport transfers, personalised check-in, a dedicated butler for each suite, access to The Club Lounge, in-suite plunge pools and other top-end amenities.

No two dining experiences at The Leela are ever alike. Jamavar, the hotel's signature restaurant, impresses with a marvellous array of gourmet Indian and Goan food in an ambience made all the more memorable by its décor, which features rare, antique Jamavar shawls.

If you are not in the mood for sumptuous Indian cuisine, the resort has several other options to tempt you. How about Italian fare

with a Mediterranean twist at The Riverside? Set against the backdrop of the River Sal with the mellow glow of the evening sun in the horizon, dinner promises to be a completely unforgettable experience. The view is equally breathtaking at Susegado, the seafood grill by the beach.

The Café, with its extensive choice of Western and Asian dishes, is ideal for guests with varying food preferences. Living

up to its reputation as the place for discerning gourmets, The Club Lounge mesmerises with tantalising fusion cuisine amidst ultra-hip and tasteful surrounds.

Aqua is the gathering place for lovers of fine wines, cognacs, malt whiskies and cigars. It is a popular venue for both business and leisure, and the mood gets decidedly more charged when the house lights dim, the strobe lights come on, and

THIS PAGE: Discerning travellers appreciate the exclusivity which comes with The Club at The Leela. The one-bedroom suites are contemporary in design and elegantly styled.

OPPOSITE: Spend a romantic evening under the stars at The Riverside, renowned for its Italian fare.

top-of-the-charts music blares over the speakers. Guests who are keen on people-watching or being in the thick of the action will vouch that the dance floor at Aqua is the hottest place to be any time of the year.

Goa, with its long stretches of unspoilt, golden-sand beaches, is affectionately known as the beach capital of India. Living up to this reputation, The Leela has a wide variety of water sports to offer guests, including fishing, parasailing, jet-skiing, wakeboarding, dolphin and sunset cruises, speedboat rides and much more.

A 12-hole golf course is set within gardens overlooking the palm-fringed beach, and is ideal for golfers who want to improve their short game.

With so many activities to pursue, it can be a challenge to find the time for a session at the spa, but many guests do their best to make the time in order to experience the range of Ayurvedic and holistic treatments available. The menu does not end there,

however. Other treatments are also offered, along with meditation and yoga.

Goa is located in an area rich in culture and history, and nature abounds. In the vicinity of The Leela are parks, monuments and relics of great interest to both casual and specialist visitors. Aside from beautiful beaches like Calangute, Colva and Benaulim, there are several renowned wildlife and bird sanctuaries.

Old Goa is home to Baroque churches like Church of Our Lady of the Immaculate Conception, Basilica of Bom Jesus and Se Cathedral, each bearing fine architectural details which have survived the test of time. Well-known temples include Sri Shantadurga and Sri Mangesh. Goan heritage is peppered with stories of brave battles fought to defend the motherland, and Fort Aguada, with its lighthouse and infamous jail, has more than its fair share of tales to tell.

Those looking for an ideal beach holiday will not be disappointed with The Leela, Goa.

PHOTOGRAPHS COURTESY OF THE LEELA, GOA.

FACTS		
ROOMS		54 Pavilion Rooms • 74 Lagoon Suites • 4 Lagoon Deluxe Suites • 4 Royal Villas • 15 Club Suites • 1 Presidential Suite
FOOD		Jamavar: Indian and Goan • The Café: Western and Asian • The Riverside Restaurant: Italian • Susegado: grilled seafood • The Club Lounge: fusion
DRINK		The Pool Bar • Aqua
FEATURES		pool • spa • fitness centre • tennis club • golf course • water sports
BUSINESS		meeting rooms • outdoor function spaces • business centre • secretarial services
NEARBY		Aguada and Terekhol forts • Museum of Christian Art • Braganza House • beaches
CONTACT		Cavelossim, Mobor, Goa 403731 • telephone: +91.83.2287 1234 • facsimile: +91.83.1287 1352 • email: leela@ghmhotels.com • website: www.theleela.com

The Leela Kempinski, Mumbai

Bustling, dynamic and fast-paced, Mumbai is the vibrant commercial centre of India. In the midst of such frenetic activity sits The Leela Kempinski, Mumbai, offering a sanctuary to harried business people and a haven to those seeking quietude.

The hotel is located within beautifully landscaped grounds with serene ponds, cascading fountains, lush greenery and cheery floral blooms. Guests are invited to lose themselves in the embrace of nature, to cast aside the stresses of the city and have them replaced by calm and quiet.

No matter how many times guests pass through it, the lobby never fails to impress. Words like opulent, stunning and magnificent naturally come to mind at its sight. A grand dome with an ethnic roof of beaten gold leaf soars three storeys high; colonnaded structures feature on each level, around which exotic plants have been artfully placed, while muted lights cast a golden glow on the whole area.

The Leela Kempinski prides itself on its balance of the old and new, boasting the most up to date amenities and services within a hotel so evocative of India's mystique and traditions, yet being the only hotel in the city with a resort feel.

Every room and suite is outfitted with the modern conveniences expected by today's travellers. But the hotel differentiates itself

...a décor best described as modern grandeur...

from others with just that little bit more—10 different room categories, 100-channel cable TV, and state-of-the-art technology, among other things.

With each refurbishment, the hotel scales newer heights in caring for its guests. The contemporary feel of the Deluxe Rooms is augmented by sophisticated offerings such as plasma TVs, massage showerheads and daylight shower rooms—the epitome of modernity and creativity in a city hotel.

The two top floors are taken up by The Privilege Club rooms and suites. True to its name, guests here enjoy exclusive check-in and check-out services, the use of meeting facilities and the business centre, and the attention of a personal butler.

The exclusive Club rooms stand out because of carefully designed details such as computerised amenities which are operable from a bedside digital panel and complimentary broadband Internet access. The well-appointed private lounge is a cosy venue stocked with hot snacks and refreshments—great for a quick perk-me-up, or informal discussions and meetings, while the library offers a rich source of information for both casual reading and research.

Many guests have raved about the peerless service and new look of the rooms, and just as many have become loyal followers of the delectable cuisine served at its speciality restaurants.

Jamavar imparts the varied tastes savoured by the royal families of India over the centuries. In this restaurant, which has a décor best described as modern grandeur, the chefs have created a menu comprising the best recipes from the country's many palaces, including spicy Mughlai dishes.

Guests who enjoy fine dining will love Stella, the Italian speciality restaurant. Fans

THIS PAGE (FROM LEFT): Guests planning a long-term stay will appreciate the comforts of a Deluxe Suite; mirrors help to create a more spacious feel in the bathrooms; the Premier Club Rooms epitomise contemporary style.

OPPOSITE: The use of lighting and colour create a vibrant atmosphere around the pool.

of Chinese food have the option of Hunan, Sichuan or Cantonese dishes at The Great Wall. All-day dining is available at Citrus, the brasserie with an eye-catching 'food theatre' and an assortment of dishes from around the world.

When darkness descends, the hotel's Zaha lounge bar, with its two dance floors, is a magnet for the young and young at heart. Sporting metallic hues of silver and grey, with splashes of strong fuchsia and purple, the lounge is decidedly avant-garde

in design and hip in appeal. A more sedate alternative to the eclectic Zaha is the Lobby Lounge, a quiet niche in the lobby where cocktails are served.

The Leela Kempinski is outstanding in many areas, including meeting facilities. The Grand Ballroom has a capacity of up to 2,000 for sit-down dinners, and is the largest banquet space in the city. There are several other function rooms of varying sizes.

Sports and wellness are important lifestyle requisites, and these are adequately

THIS PAGE: Enjoy drinks al fresco at 6 Degrees.

OPPOSITE (FROM TOP): The simple and well-lit décor of Citrus makes it ideal for casual meals; Jamavar impresses with its sumptuous Indian cuisine.

photo opportunities offered by the Gateway of India, a majestic yellow basalt stone structure built to commemorate the visit of King George V and Queen Mary, or learn about the history of India at the Prince of Wales Museum. Also within the vicinity of the hotel are other places of interest such as the Haji Ali Shrine and Elephanta Caves.

provided for by the hotel. An outdoor swimming pool awaits those who love the combination of sun and water, while a slow stroll through the hotel's lovely gardens is always a great way to start or end the day. The fully-equipped gym and squash court are available for workouts in air-conditioned comfort. From yoga to massages, hair styling to shopping, everything is conveniently located on the hotel's premises.

Beyond The Leela Kempinski, guests with time to spare can take advantage of the

FACTS		
	ROOMS	289 Deluxe and Deluxe Premiere Rooms • 24 Parlour Deluxe Rooms • 18 Executive Suites • 6 Deluxe Suites • 75 Privilege Club Rooms • 6 Privilege Club Executive Suites • 1 Privilege Club Deluxe Suite • 4 Presidential Suites
	FOOD	Jamavar: Indian • The Great Wall: Chinese • Stella: Italian • Citrus: international
	DRINK	Zaha • Lobby Lounge • The Bar
	BUSINESS	Internet access • meeting rooms • business centre • secretarial services
	FEATURES	pool • health club and fitness centre • squash • shops
	NEARBY	Gateway of India • Haji Ali Shrine • Elephanta Caves • Prince of Wales Museum • Juhu Beach • Bandra Shopping Centre
	CONTACT	Sahar, Mumbai 400059, Maharashtra • telephone: +91.22.5691 1234 • facsimile: +91.22.5691 1212 • email: reservations@theleela.com • website: www.theleela.com

PHOTOGRAPHS COURTESY OF THE LEELA KEMPINSKI, MUMBAI.

The Oberoi, Mumbai

Mumbai, India's largest city, buzzes with a vibrancy and life that cannot be found anywhere else. It is home to India's film industry, affectionately known as 'Bollywood', the country's media industry, and is the centre of its financial institutes, and Mumbai-dwellers are not wrong to consider their city the 'Big Apple' of India. This is where visitors will find a confluence of international conglomerates, thriving industries and the country's busiest airport. Mumbai also offers the best introduction to India's modern metropolis through the amazing Oberoi experience.

From cosy airport lounges managed by the award-winning hotel chain to immigration and customs clearance, mobile phones, newspapers and chauffeured limousines, every little travel detail is handled for you with ease. At The Oberoi, Mumbai, every guest is treated as an honoured VIP.

The Oberoi is a business traveller's dream: efficient, wired and quietly elegant, with clever corners and seating areas for private discussions. The hotel's 24-hour butler service is the one feature among many often singled out by guests for praise.

THIS PAGE (FROM TOP): Mumbai's skyline sometimes draws comparisons with the iconic skyline of Manhattan; the hotel's lobby exemplifies simple, contemporary elegance.

OPPOSITE: Wake up to an ocean view from the comfortable confines of a Deluxe Room.

Guests are usually surprised by the generous room sizes of this city hotel, but as a leader in the industry, The Oberoi is comfortable with breaking the mould, especially to benefit its guests. Along with spectacular views from the windows, each room and suite is designed for functionality and luxury. All the rooms and suites are located around a central atrium, with outer views over the city, bay or ocean, depending on the room chosen.

The lavish Kohinoor Suite has hosted celebrities, movie stars and heads-of-state from around the world. Modern and classic décor meet here. The opulence extends to the exclusive jacuzzi and sauna which have gold-plated bathroom fittings and amenities custom-fitted to guests' preferences. For those guests whose discussions must remain top secret, there is a designated 'safe' work area in the suite.

People in search of excellent food inevitably end up dining at The Oberoi. With its evolving range of cuisines, a superb wine list and great ambience, it is easy to understand why. Northwestern Indian cuisine is the focus at Kandahar, while Tiffin showcases a menu of healthy, light items inspired by Pacific Rim and Indian dishes. The hotel's latest offering, Vetro, serves Italian cuisine. Drop by The Bayview Bar after dinner for fine malt whiskies or a Cuban cigar.

The Oberoi has made a name for itself when it comes to top-of-the-line business facilities, but just as outstanding are its health and leisure facilities, including The Oberoi Spa and Fitness Centre by Banyan Tree and its large shopping arcade. Such facilities ensure guests never have to leave the hotel if they do not want to.

Sealing a deal on the green? The golf course is a short car ride away. Also within minutes of The Oberoi, Mumbai are squash and tennis centres, as well as numerous heritage buildings and places of interest.

PHOTOGRAPHS COURTESY OF THE OBEROI, MUMBAI.

FACTS

ROOMS	95 Superior Rooms • 140 Premium Rooms • 76 Deluxe Rooms • 11 Executive Suites • 6 Deluxe Suites • 4 Presidential Suites • 1 Kohinoor Suite
FOOD	Tiffin: Pacific Rim, Japanese and Indian • Kandahar: Indian • Vetro: Italian • The Tea Lounge: pastries and savouries
DRINK	The Bayview Bar
FEATURES	The Oberoi Spa and Fitness Centre by Banyan Tree • hair salon • shopping arcade
BUSINESS	high-speed Internet access • business centre • meeting rooms
NEARBY	Gateway of India • Prince of Wales Museum • golf • horseback riding
CONTACT	Nariman Point, Mumbai 400021, Maharashtra • telephone: +91.22.5632 5757 • facsimile: +91.22.5632 4142 • email: reservations@oberoi-mumbai.com • website: www.oberoihotels.com

The Taj Mahal Palace + Tower, Mumbai

One impressive property with two wings of very different appeal, The Taj Mahal Palace + Tower, Mumbai ranks among the finest hotels in the world.

Its popularity goes beyond its strategic location. The hotel has a proud history dating back more than a century, and some things have never changed—the close attention to detail, superb service and its preferred venue status.

The Taj Mahal Palace, built in 1903 and carefully restored, wears its Moorish, Oriental and Florentine styles with pride. Rising majestically from the banks of Mumbai Harbour, right next to the Gateway of India, it is a constant reminder of the subcontinent's glorious heritage. The iconic Taj Mahal Tower was erected in 1972.

The grandiose interior of The Taj Mahal Palace is a feast for the senses. Priceless genuine artefacts and antiques are placed along the corridors and public spaces for all to admire. Guests are usually pleasantly surprised to come across an old Belgian chandelier or a Goan Christian *objet d'art*, collected over the years.

The liberal use of wood, exquisite hand-woven carpets and rich hues add to the lavish interior of The Taj Mahal Palace. One of the most eye-catching features of this wing—and there are many—is the cantilever stairway. Set against the muted lights and

THIS PAGE: The magnificent Taj Mahal Palace + Tower takes pride of place next to the historic Gateway of India.

OPPOSITE (FROM TOP): The hotel's lobby is formal, yet evokes a sense of comfort; enjoy Eastern Mediterranean cuisine at Souk.

curved lines of the multi-archways, it is reminiscent of a bygone era, when royalty resided within these premises.

Each exclusive suite at The Taj Mahal Palace is uniquely and lovingly furnished, and features period furniture, one-of-a-kind paintings, luxuriant textures and plush rugs. The result is a guestroom fit for for a king. The stunning Presidential Suite comes with a high-domed ceiling, expansive sitting room and separate work area. The best of traditional architecture blends seamlessly with modern conveniences here.

The Taj Club Rooms are a favourite with frequent travellers. Functional, large and comfortable, each room comes equipped

with the latest in telecommunications technology. The Taj Club is a great place at which to unwind after a hard day at work; it is also a venue well suited to the negotiation of contracts and sealing deals, albeit in an informal setting.

Luxury is the common theme running through The Taj Mahal Tower as well. The winning combination of luminous alabaster ceilings, onyx columns and floors inlaid with semi-precious stones never fails to elicit gasps of admiration—a reaction which is certainly well deserved.

Guestrooms at The Taj Mahal Tower exude a modern appeal and style all of their own. Residents on the higher floors enjoy splendid views of the harbourfront and sea, or the cosmopolitan cityscape.

The restaurants at The Taj Mahal Palace + Tower are legendary for their variety of cuisines from around the world. The Zodiac Grill is recognised as one of the finest restaurants in the country. Daily, the highly-accomplished chefs oversee the preparation of an array of delectable international gourmet dishes, all of which are enhanced by the appropriate pairing of vintage wines.

The myriad flavours of India are brought to the fore at Masala Kraft, where recipes for traditional Indian fare are polished to

perfection, and then given a modern twist. A must-try is Wasabi by Morimoto, one of India's finest Japanese restaurants. The Chinese restaurant, Golden Dragon, is well known for its spicy Sichuan food, while Souk offers exotic cuisines such as Lebanese, Moroccan, Turkish and Greek. For all-day dining and meals served in a casual setting, head to Shamiana, and if a light snack is what you are looking for, try The Sea Lounge. If a relaxing drink after work or dinner is what you are after, try the elegant Harbour Bar, where a selection of Martinis, Champagnes and cigars are offered against the backdrop of the Gateway of India.

Mumbai's active pace does not slow when the day draws to a close, it merely moves indoors. Insomnia at The Taj Mahal Palace + Tower is where the 'in' crowd naturally gravitates to. Two themed bars— where exciting cocktails are concocted— and a massive dance floor provide plentiful opportunities for fun and entertainment.

A sure way to recover after all that partying is with a visit to Jiva Spa. Choose from an extensive spa menu, and trained therapists will knead, massage and restore your body, mind and spirit. Day packages are available here, as are yoga sessions conducted by trained instructors.

THIS PAGE (CLOCKWISE FROM BELOW): **The stately and expansive Presidential Suite; vibrant colours and ornate fittings reflect India's royal style.**

OPPOSITE: **The main pool at The Taj Mahal Palace.**

Cutting through the waves is another good way to invigorate the senses. The Taj Luxury Yacht, an elegant vessel with three air-conditioned bedrooms, offers a great way to explore the vast Arabian Sea. No cruise is complete without a serving of canapés, chilled wine or ice-cold drinks. The yacht includes a bar and entertainment system.

Many people will attest to the effectiveness of retail therapy for a wide variety of ailments. The Taj Mahal Palace + Tower has its own shopping arcade, but if that is not enough, the hotel is just a short distance from the city centre where more shopping opportunities beckon: Courtyard, Colaba Causeway, Westside, Crossroads, Kemps Corner...the choices are plentiful.

For those who want to take in the sights of Mumbai, the Prince of Wales Museum and Jehangir Art Gallery are in the vicinity. Conveniently, four- and eight-hour city sightseeing packages are available at The Taj Mahal Palace + Tower.

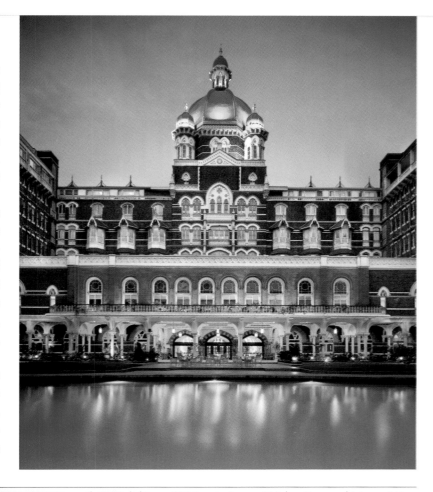

FACTS

ROOMS	The Taj Mahal Tower: 209 Superior Rooms, 68 Deluxe Rooms and 1 Luxury Suite • The Taj Mahal Palace: 24 Luxury Rooms, 134 Grande Luxury Rooms, 83 Taj Club Rooms, 22 Executive Suites, 8 Luxury Suites, 5 Junior Suites, 9 Grande Luxury Suites and 2 Presidential Suites
FOOD	The Zodiac Grill: international • Masala Kraft: Indian • Souk: Eastern Mediterranean • Wasabi: Japanese • Golden Dragon: Sichuan • The Sea Lounge: light meals
FEATURES	Jiva Spa • Taj Luxury Yacht • pool • 24-hour fitness centre • shopping arcade
BUSINESS	high-speed Wi-Fi Internet access • meeting rooms • banquet halls • business centre
CONTACT	Apollo Bunder, Mumbai 400001, Maharashtra • telephone: +91.22.5665 3366 • facsimile: +91.22.5665 0300 • email: tmhbc.bom@tajhotels.com • website: www.tajhotels.com

The Verandah in the Forest, Matheran

Located just two hours from the bustling city of Mumbai, the cool and forested highlands of Matheran were a haven to the British, who used to converge there to escape the heat of the Indian summer. Many hill stations—remnants from the colonial days—still dot the ranges; but there is only one pedestrian hill station in India, and all of Asia—Matheran. This is where you will find The Verandah in the Forest.

Guests can reach this 700-m-high (2,297-ft-high) resort by foot, on rickshaw, horseback, or in grand style on a palanquin. Built by General H. Barr in 1852, the bungalow has been lovingly restored to create an exclusive 11-room retreat with the finest amenities and standards of service.

Most of the bedrooms open directly onto a generous verandah, which inspired the name Verandah in the Forest. From this verandah, glorious views of the surroundings abound, and on a clear day, guests are assured a good view of Navi (New) Mumbai; in the evenings, the city's bright lights twinkle merrily.

The bungalow exudes an old-world grandeur with its mix of local and colonial architectural styles. Wide corridors aside,

THIS PAGE (FROM TOP): The resort offers numerous vantage points from which guests can take in the view; a wide, covered verandah runs along the front of the house.

OPPOSITE: The high ceiling of the living room is one of the property's most outstanding features.

Most of the bedrooms open directly onto a generous verandah...

the floors are covered largely with tiles from General Barr's time. As fans whirl overhead, and the same lights come on, time seems to stand still. The ambience of a luxury residence, a restful summer retreat, suffuses the property. This may explain its perpetual full occupancy since its opening.

Every room, named after a renowned personality, has a unique identity, though each one is equally comfortable and well-appointed. A large four-poster bed dominates the room, which also features antique furniture with charming upholstery. Meals are served at Malet Hall, at a long dining table which can seat up to 30 people. In this formal setting, guests will enjoy dishes from an international menu.

Red mud trails meander lazily from the property through the surrounding forest. Guests usually enjoy taking long walks in the cool air, heading towards the numerous lookouts dotting the hillside. Charlotte Lake, which touches the property, has been a source of water for the resort since the early days, and it continues to be so today. Guests are free to take a walk down to this picturesque lake and enjoy a picnic by the water. The Kapadia Market is an ideal place for bargain hunters to pick up mementos, while the Parsi Cemetery is where many of the area's finest citizens have been laid to rest. In fact, some of the rooms at the hotel are named after them.

FACTS

ROOMS	11 rooms
FOOD	international
FEATURES	indoor games
NEARBY	Charlotte Lake • Louisa Point • Alexander Point • Mount Barry • Lumley Seat • Simpson's Tank • Rugby Hotel • Kapadia Market • Adamji's Bungalow • Parsi Cemetery • trekking • horseback riding
CONTACT	Barr House, Matheran 410102, District Raigarh, Maharashtra • telephone: +91.2148.230 296 • facsimile: +91.2148.230 811 • email: sales@neemranahotels.com • website: www.neemranahotels.com

PHOTOGRAPHS COURTESY OF THE VERANDAH IN THE FOREST, MATHERAN.

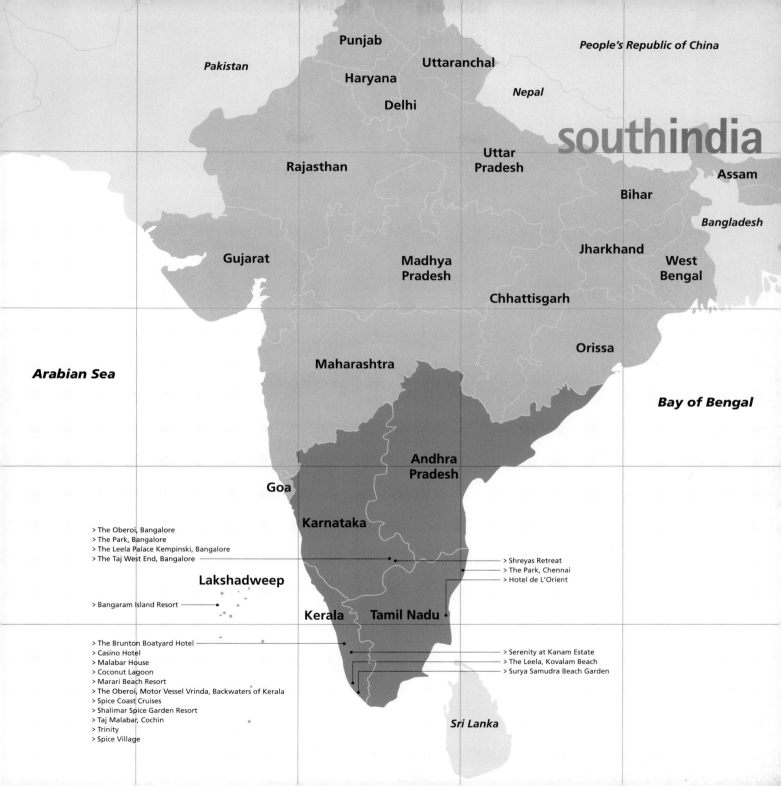

Punjab

Pakistan

Haryana

Uttaranchal

People's Republic of China

Delhi

Nepal

southindia

Rajasthan

Uttar
Pradesh

Assam

Bihar

Bangladesh

Gujarat

Madhya
Pradesh

Jharkhand

West
Bengal

Chhattisgarh

Orissa

Arabian Sea

Maharashtra

Bay of Bengal

Andhra
Pradesh

Goa

> The Oberoi, Bangalore
> The Park, Bangalore
> The Leela Palace Kempinski, Bangalore
> The Taj West End, Bangalore

Karnataka

> Shreyas Retreat
> The Park, Chennai
> Hotel de L'Orient

Lakshadweep

> Bangaram Island Resort

Kerala   Tamil Nadu

> The Brunton Boatyard Hotel
> Casino Hotel
> Malabar House
> Coconut Lagoon
> Marari Beach Resort
> The Oberoi, Motor Vessel Vrinda, Backwaters of Kerala
> Spice Coast Cruises
> Shalimar Spice Garden Resort
> Taj Malabar, Cochin
> Trinity
> Spice Village

> Serenity at Kanam Estate
> The Leela, Kovalam Beach
> Surya Samudra Beach Garden

Sri Lanka

incandescent and resplendent

They are known as the four sisters of the Indian peninsula and cut an indelible swathe across nearly 70 per cent of India's land mass, with a 5,700-km (3,542-mile) coastline along the Arabian Sea and the Bay of Bengal.

These states—Tamil Nadu, Karnataka, Andhra Pradesh and Kerala—enjoy vastly differing topography and are home to a variety of vegetation and wildlife. They explode with the riotous colours that are the leitmotifs of India. This visual legacy is written in scarlet, the colour of the Indian *tilak*, the mark on the forehead with which Indians welcome their guests; jade, the colour of its forests and paddy fields; saffron, the hue of ripening corn and post-monsoon sunsets; and chestnut, reflected in the sands and newly irrigated land.

The people of these four states are champions of a proud heritage, the Dravidian ethnic and linguistic tradition that predates Aryan northern India (4000–3000 BC) by an estimated 1,000 years. Yet, they are the ultimate repositories and guardians of India's Vedic culture which originated from the lighter-skinned pastoral people of the northern and northwestern Indo-Gangetic plains. The culture and belief systems that travelled from north to south were protected from invaders from Asia Minor and Central Asia, to whom much of northern India fell prey. To a large extent the people of the south were protected by India's great divide, the Vindhya Mountains. This range runs east to west, separating the fertile river valley of the Ganges River from the Deccan Plateau, which occupies much of the Indian peninsula. On these plains lie the best beaches of the subcontinent, and on the periphery of the Western and Eastern Ghats are the lands of tea, coffee and spice.

Beyond these mountains, in the wedge-shaped plateau, are great old cities supported by rich farm lands and a culture that has its roots in the Dravidian (south Indian) family of languages. The four sister states have been carved out on the basis of predominance of the four major Dravidian languages—Tamil, Telegu, Kannada and Malayalam.

PAGE 160: Kerala's backwaters are one of south India's most well-known sights.

THIS PAGE (FROM TOP): **Here as elsewhere in India, Bollywood reigns;** tilak *for sale in the market.*

OPPOSITE: **The colours of the south's temples express the region's diversity.**

guardian angels

After the decline of the Gupta Empire in 550 AD, during India's Golden Age, the classical patterns of civilisation continued to thrive in the Deccan and in southern India, which acquired a more prominent place in history. The rulers of the south patronised all three religions to which India gave birth—Buddhism, Hinduism and Jainism. The proponents of these religions vied with each other for royal favour, which was expressed in land grants, but more importantly in the creation of monumental temples. By the mid-7th century, Buddhism and Jainism began to decline as sectarian Hindu devotional cults of Shiva and Vishnu competed vigorously for popular support.

A visit to the south may well coincide with one of the many magnificent festivals which are celebrated with any number of classic southern dance forms. The *bharata natyam*—prayer and meditation in motion—is now performed on world stages, while the *kathakali* mask dance depicting divine tales, the clash of gods and demons and beasts of Indian legend, and the graceful *kalaipattu*, the martial art of Kerala, draw interminable applause when performed at festivals overseas.

Visitors who want to experience the classical music and dance traditions of this region should head south between mid-December to mid-January for the immensely popular annual Festival of Carnatic Music and Dance.

THIS PAGE AND OPPOSITE (TOP RIGHT):
From the famous kathakali to classical dance, India's south embodies all that is vibrant and colourful about the subcontinent.

OPPOSITE (CENTRE AND BELOW): Shop for textiles while in Tamil Nadu; brand new cars await export at Chennai's port.

tamils in the cyber age

Tamil Nadu and its capital Chennai are developing rapidly in the areas of economy, human resource, social advancement and culture. Tamil Nadu is one of the top three Indian states that enjoys the highest foreign investment in sectors including automobiles, information technology and telecommunications. The cities of Bangalore (in Karnataka) and Hyderabad (in Andhra Pradesh), too, are quickly establishing themselves as technological nerve centres and are visited regularly by foreign leaders and industry heavyweights such as Bill Gates. High-rises, multi-cuisine restaurants, Internet cafés,

nightclubs where the music never stops and space-age movie theatres are *de rigueur*. But agriculture is still the mainstay of life for about three-quarters of the population. Tamil Nadu is equally rich in crafts such as handloomed silk, metalwork, leather goods, *kalamkari* (traditional hand-painted fabric using natural dyes), brass, bronze and copper ware, carved wood, palm leaf and cane articles.

With a heady mixture of formidable monuments, an incandescent culture, a rich history, distinctive beaches and resplendent skies in which the sun never seems to set, and world-class conference facilities, Tamil Nadu is a made-to-order destination for incentive groups hungry for culture and an enticing environment within which to talk global business. The eastern and western ends of the state are defined by Point Calimere and Mudumalai National Park, while the northern tip is Pulicat Lake and the southernmost stop is Kanyakumari, also known as Cape Comorin—India's fabled Land's End.

romancing chennai

Chennai bustles, buzzes and hums with vibrancy and an unparalleled architectural legacy. It is the epicentre of the Hindu tradition, and is India's fourth-largest metropolis and the third most important port city. It expresses both the tenacious devoutness and the artistic skills of the Tamil people as well as their heady swallow-dive into the

modern world. Most of its Tamil-speaking inhabitants speak and read English. Points of interest, especially for the traveller with a tight schedule, are the Vedantangal Bird Sanctuary, the indescribably ornate Sri Meenakshi Temple complex of Madurai, and the Alagar Hills, home to the Tirupparakunram Rock Temple.

The city's most prominent landmark is Fort St George, built in 1640, where the British East India Company housed its garrisons. In modern day India, this edifice is now the seat of the Secretariat and Legislative Assembly. The flagstaff that now flies the Indian tricolour flag is a 14-m-high (46-ft-high) pole that was recovered from a 17th-century shipwreck. History and souvenir buffs should visit the museum that is part of the fort's interior. At the end of the 17th century, British architects built St Mary's Church, recognised as Chennai's first English church and India's oldest surviving British church.

Moving from Christianity to Hinduism in this historical state takes less than a hop, skip and jump. Just as St Mary's Church is the city's oldest church, the Shiva Kapaleeshwarar Temple in Mylapore is Chennai's oldest temple. In dramatic juxtaposition, right beside this monument to Lord Shiva rises the San Thome Cathedral which, according to legend, contains the remains of St Thomas the Apostle.

tickling the tastebuds

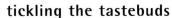

Chennai is a mecca of vegetarian cooking, but it also caters to exclusive gourmet tastes. One such great eatery is Arirang (its name is derived from an old Korean song), owned by a Korean lady, Park Young Ja. With Korean music playing over a surround-sound system and sunken seating arrangements, it is a favourite haunt of corporate executives from Hyundai, LG, Samsung and Daewoo. Some recommended dishes to try here are pork and seafood, fried or barbecued at your table.

At the Dhabba Express—a split-level courtyard like a Mexican *hacienda*—expect authentic Punjabi cuisine. Foodies can eat to their heart's content with just a little more than US$1. The seating arrangement comprises *charpoys* (bunks made of knotted rope), which recreate the look of India's roadside *dhabas*—highway truck stops where you can recline as you eat. Quicky's is India's first coffee chain, where more than 101 blends are available—including latte, espresso, mocha, cappuccino and americano—along with sandwiches and ice cream. Stalls sell various merchandise and international magazines, and the music blares all day, providing the unmistakable ambience of a crowded and bustling city.

exploring further afield

Do not just confine yourself to the city. Explore what lies beyond with a trip to Ooty, the famous hill station built by the British in the Nilgiri Hills in the 19th century as the summer headquarters of the then-Madras government. Ooty is now a popular location for filming Bollywood love scenes.

Further south is the district of Tirunelveli, where you will find the town of Kuttalam, famous for its waterfalls and health resort. This is where travellers can experience the healing properties of cascading water as it drops from a height of 91 m (299 ft).

Golf, anybody? India is fast becoming a major destination for golf holidays. In Tamil Nadu, Coimbatore's 18-hole, 6,233-m (6,817-yd), par-71 course is a magnificent facility that will please any golfer. Chennai's Madras Gymkhana Club, founded in 1886, and the Cosmopolitan Golf Annexe at Saidapet also offer greenways and fast fairways with challenging roughs and bunkers.

THIS PAGE: **The Sri Meenakshi Temple complex is among India's most famous sights.**

OPPOSITE (FROM TOP): **The south is recognised for its many temples; floral decorations add to the region's air of festivity.**

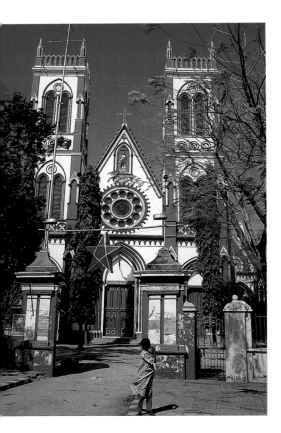

the french connection

Chennai, a big efficient metropolis, is a good centre from which to embark on a journey through southern India. About 135 km (84 miles) from Chennai is the laid-back 'French' town of Pondicherry (Pondy). This coastal town was one of the victims of the 2004 tsunami tragedy, in which 26 of its villages were battered, more than 570 people were killed and over 1,000 injured. But Pondy has recovered and still exudes a unique charm with its seashore boulevard, French colonial buildings, and the renowned Sri Aurobindo Ashram and the city of Auroville, where the meditation-inclined from all over the world seek out their private nirvanas.

Pondy covers over 492 sq km (190 sq miles) and is divided into four districts. Pondicherry town is the administrative capital of the union territory of Pondicherry, which comprises other former French enclaves in India including Karaikal in Tamil Nadu, Mahe in Kerala and Yanam in Andhra Pradesh. Believe it or not, a mind-boggling 55 languages and dialects are spoken in Pondicherry, though English, French and Tamil are the most common.

Three hundred years of French heritage is visible in the town's sprawling boulevards, sylvan promenades, street signs, spacious colonial mansions and wealth of French restaurants. Towering statues of French personalities who left their mark in Pondy include François Martin, the first administrator; J. F. Dupleix, the governor of French-India; and Madame Mirra Richard, a French painter-sculptor who was Sri Aurobindo Ghose's most ardent disciple and known as 'the Mother' who helped establish the Sri Aurobindo Ashram and Auroville. Aayi Mandapam is located in Bharathi Park in the heart of Pondy and was built in Greco-Roman style during the reign of Napoleon III, Emperor of France. Statues of Dupleix and Joan of Arc, and the Place du Gouvernement epitomise Pondy's French antecedents. A French war memorial in India? Where else but in Pondy where it is brilliantly lit on July 14, Bastille Day, each year.

THIS PAGE (TOP) AND OPPOSITE (TOP): The Église de Sacré Coeur de Jésus is an example of French-inspired architecture in Pondy, while the use of soft colours alludes to the town's colonial heritage as well.

THIS PAGE (BELOW) AND OPPOSITE (BELOW): Street signs and statues of French personalities are another French legacy.

Seventeenth- and 18th-century French evangelism created a proud Christian heritage of religious architecture all over Pondy—the Gothic Église de Sacré Coeur de Jésus, the Église de Notre Dame de la Conception Imaculée and the Église de Notre Dame des Anges. As the abode of a myriad of faiths, much like Chennai, Pondicherry is also dotted with about 350 temples, some of which were built by the Hindu Chola kings between the 10th and 12th centuries. The Sri Gokilambal Thirukameswara Temple is architecturally among the most outstanding. During May and June, this magnificently preserved monument is the backdrop of the 10-day Brahmotsavam festival, when a 15-m-high (49-ft-high) chariot bedecked in marigolds and painted with all the colours of the rainbow leads a merry procession of religious revellers. In a peculiar French tribute to secularism, French governors used to join the Hindu procession. Today, Pondicherry's Indian lieutenant-governor continues that proud tradition.

Shopping in Pondy is a unique experience. It is a treasure trove of handicrafts, including pottery, leather and handmade paper, most of which come from Auroville, a city begun by 'the Mother' in an effort to create an international home, a place no nation could lay claim to.

Pondicherry's cuisine is as varied as anywhere in the south, but French food is one of the highlights. One place that is usually recommended is Rendezvous, where guests can enjoy their meal on the rooftop or in the classic French country dining room. Though the menu is primarily French, guests also have a choice of Indian, Chinese and Western dishes such as burgers and pizza.

Also popular with both locals and tourists is Satsanga, located in the garden of a colonial house. Though ideal for a casual lunch or dinner, it is the restaurant's breakfasts that many come back for. Feast on tantalising omelettes, crêpes and freshly baked bread, or a simple bowl of muesli and yoghurt. After breakfast, head to the beaches for a lazy afternoon. Serenity Beach in the north lives up to its name, and Paradise Beach, to the south, is where you can do water sports and enjoy boat cruises. Pondy's waters are also a great place to catch a glimpse of friendly dolphins.

cruising into karnataka

With its resplendent palaces, ancient monuments, verdant paddy fields, sandalwood trees, modern cities and vibrant nightlife, Karnataka is a distinctly south Indian state, and showcases the best of traditional and contemporary India.

The state is one of the wettest areas in India, with the coastal regions receiving the bulk of the southwest monsoon rains from June till September. The mountainous Western Ghats, which run parallel to the coast, hinder the rains from moving inland, and so the interiors are much drier. The entire state enjoys great weather from October to March, with a few spells of rain brought by the northeast monsoon.

Most of its 45 million inhabitants—called Kannadigas—speak the Kannada language, with its ancient inflections that sound like Greek to the rest of India's one billion inhabitants.

the wonders of hampi

Historical ruins and monuments are visual expressions of Karnataka's history of Buddhist, Hindu and Muslim dynasties including the ruins of Hampi, a World Heritage Site. The 14th-century city, once the seat of the famed Vijayanagar Empire, now leaves visitors awe-struck with its landscape of large boulders.

The ruins live to tell a tale of glory perhaps unmatched in world architecture. Scattered over a 26-sq-km (10-sq-mile) area, the splendid remains of palaces and gateways conjure images of man's infinite talent, creativity and wealth, surpassing anything you can imagine. The most splendid monument of Hampi is undoubtedly the Vittala Temple Complex with its 56 'musical' pillars—they reverberate when tapped. To the east of the hall is the famous stone chariot with stone wheels that actually revolve. In front of the shrine stands the great *mandapa*. Published archaeological sources describe it as an arc 'resting on a richly sculpted basement, its roof supported by huge pillars of granite about 4.6 m (15 ft) in height, each consisting of a central pillar surrounded by detached shafts, all cut from one single block of stone. Several of the

THIS PAGE AND OPPOSITE: The once glorious city of Hampi is now a landscape of ruins in boulders. Keep an eye out for the magnificent stone chariot.

carved pillars were attacked with such fury that they are hardly more than shapeless blocks of stones, and a large portion of the central part has been destroyed utterly.'

Hampi is also full of surprises like the King's Balance, where kings were weighed against grain, gold or money which was then distributed to the poor, and the Queen's Bath, a swimming pool with arched corridors, projecting balconies and fountains that spouted perfumed water.

the scent of mysore

Karnataka is also known as the capital of *agarbathi* (incense sticks), especially those perfumed with jasmine, rose and particularly sandalwood. But if you want the original stuff, the kind that can be used for aromatherapy, visit Mysore's sandalwood oil factory. The city is known for this product, and it is well worth spending a little more and getting the real deal.

The Maharaja's Palace is another highlight of the city. It has been drawing millions of tourists from all over the world with its riches of stained glass, mirrors, mosaic

floors and vibrant colours. Within the palace grounds are Hindu temples such as the Shweta Varahaswamy Temple, noted for its Dravidian gateway which influenced the style of the Sri Chamundeswari Temple on Chamundi Hill.

the lure of bangalore

Bangalore, the capital of Karnataka, with its chrome-and-glass office buildings contrasting with flower gardens and parks, is often described as India's 'Garden City' and 'air-conditioned city'. It is a metropolis on the move: young women ply back and forth on motorcycles, pubs dot the city, and multi-national corporations are establishing branches and headquarters here—the Intel corporation has one of its largest research and development centres in the city, and Microsoft has opened its fourth research centre here as well.

Any good tourist guidebook will tell you that the food on offer in this city is worth the trip—seafood at Mirch restaurant, multi-cuisine at Hypnos and Indi Joe, Oriental cuisine at Mahjong Room, Memories of China and Shiok, Continental fare at Jockey Club and Bangalore Bistro, and 24-hour coffee shops like Potluck, Monsoon and Orange County. But come nightfall, Bangalore's revellers head for its famous pubs—

THIS PAGE (FROM TOP): **Hampi's elephant stables will make an impression; colourful Islamic hats await buyers outside Jama Masjid in Bangalore.**
OPPOSITE: **The fishing nets of Cochin are now iconic.**

NASA, The Pub World, Guzzlers Inn, Dublin, Nineteen Twelve and Ego's. For jazz lovers there is A Pinch of Jazz, serving Cajun and Creole cuisine to the rhythms of Armstrong, Brubeck and Shakti, and the Modern Jazz Quartet.

Apart from tippling memories, visitors to Bangalore can take home unique gifts and souvenirs in the form of pure silk scarves and wraps, ivory carvings and Lambani tribal jewellery. For these and more, check out the shops along MG Road.

kerala on the sea

Legend has it that Kerala was created when Parasuram, the sixth incarnation of Lord Vishnu, the preserver of the Hindu Trinity, stood on a mountain top and plunged his axe far into the sea, commanding the waters to retreat. The land that emerged is said to be Kerala. This southwestern state is the most verdant of all the Indian states, and is an extremely popular destination for adventure and health-related tourism, with pure air, dense tropical forests, impressive beaches and lagoons, rich vegetation and, of course, renowed backwaters. Kerala is a 560-km-long (348-mile-long) narrow stretch of land, and even its widest point is a mere 120 km (75 miles) from the sea to the mountains.

In the wet and verdant Periyar Wildlife Sanctuary, monkeys screech and chatter in areas reminiscent of the Amazon. In the backwaters between Alleppey and Quilon, farmers, mostly women in colourful skirts and blouses, toil gently in emerald fields of paddy among coconut groves and in spice plantations redolent of cardamom and clove. The Allepey backwaters have already earned the state the nickname 'Venice of the East' in international tourist circles.

Kerala has shades of Vietnam, Thailand, Cambodia and Myanmar. But the Nilgiri Hills, with their gentle slopes and tea plantations, are always there to remind you that you are in Kerala, an ancient crossroads of cultures. Here, fishing nets rest like giant, transparent butterflies on sparkling sands; synagogues, forts, churches, temples and palaces carve themselves into the memory; and distinctive customs, art forms and festivals live on, protected by the dense Western Ghats.

letting loose and letting go

The Portuguese were the first to colonise the region, followed by the Dutch, the French and finally the British. Its capital is Thiruvananthapuram, formerly known as Trivandrum. In its immediate vicinity is the gorgeous Sri Padmanabhaswamy Temple and the fascinating Napier Museum, which was built in the 19th century. This Indo-Saracenic structure houses a rare collection of archaeological and historic artefacts, bronze idols, ancient ornaments, a temple chariot and ivory carvings.

The regional diversity within this state is astounding—whitewater rafting, trekking, camping, para-gliding, mountain biking, backwater cruises and jungle safaris are yours for the picking, and one activity is never more than a few hours away from the other. The state has three main geographical regions: the coastal lowlands to the east, the fertile midlands, and the highlands, which slope down from the Western Ghats and rise to an average height of 900 m (2,953 ft), with a number of peaks well over 1,800 m (5,905 ft). On these slopes, tea, coffee, rubber and spices bless farmers with their abundance and perfume the hills with their aromas. The midlands yield a smorgasbord of crops—cashew nuts, coconuts, cassava (tapioca), bananas, rice, ginger, pepper, sugarcane and assorted vegetables.

In Kerala, simply breathing and taking in the sights is akin to relaxation, and the state's traditions buttress this laid-back, languorous mood by offering tension-banishing massages and treatments based on the natural health science of Ayurveda, a system that has been passed down through the generations since 1500 BC or even earlier.

escaping the cities

If quietude and bliss are what you are after, then head to Kottayam and the nearby town of Kumarakom, where you will find mangrove forests, paddy fields and coconut groves interspersed with enchanting waterways and canals adorned with white lilies. Floating blissfully on the waters of Vembanad Lake, your worries and the stresses of the world will dissipate. Country-made boats and canoes will transport passengers across this peaceful little universe. Nearby resorts offer Ayurvedic massages, yoga, fishing and swimming in one of the most pollution-free wetlands in the world.

If you need a retreat a little further away, head to the Lakshadweep Islands, southwest off the coast of Kerala, and home to about 55,000 people. This is an archipelago of 36 coral islands of which 10 are inhabited. One of them, Minicoy, was dubbed 'an island of females' by Marco Polo because it is home to a matriarchal society. On Bangaram Island, get a beach hut and spend your days relaxing on soft sands, eating barbecued fish and falling asleep to the sound of the waves.

the call of the temple

Nowhere in India can you escape temples. They astound and fascinate, and each has a story that can rouse you out of the most stubborn state of boredom. So it is with the Irinjalakuda Koodalmanikyam Temple dedicated to Lord Bharatha, the brother of Lord Rama. Situated 10 km (6.2 miles) away from Irinjalakuda railway station and 21 km (13 miles) from Thrissur, it is perhaps the only temple in India with Lord Bharatha as the deity.

Guruvayur, 33 km (21 miles) northwest of Thrissur, is among the most hallowed pilgrim centres in Kerala. Its Sri Krishna Temple, built in the 16^(th) century, is believed to have healing powers, and is often used for weddings and other important family events.

sands of time

Kerala is not as well-known as Goa for its beaches, perhaps because Keralites take their own beaches for granted, or like to keep them a secret from prowling tourists. Actually, the lush state has 600 km (373 miles) of coastline adorned by isolated beaches where people may not have ventured as yet. Some

THIS PAGE: You cannnot journey through Kerala without bumping into a temple.
OPPOSITE (FROM TOP): A stay in a luxurious houseboat is the way to see Kerala's backwaters; festivals abound in this state.

even have historical significance. For example, the Kodungalore coast near Cochin (or Kochi) was where St Thomas, the first missionary on the Indian coast, landed. Vasco da Gama, the Portuguese discoverer who spearheaded the European incursion into India, was marooned at Kappad near Kozhikode (previously Calicut).

Kerala's most famous crescent-shaped beach attraction, Kovalam, is picture-postcard perfect. It is ringed by groves of coconut trees unlike any other tourist beach destination in the world. The beach has two coves, Lighthouse Beach and Hawah Beach, in the vicinity of which a good number of resorts can be found, including The Leela, Kovalam Beach. Also nearby are Ayurvedic, non-invasive medicinal resorts like Surya Samudra.

andhra, the great gateway

Andhra Pradesh is a land of plateau, ravines, forests and rocks that could be part of the moonscape. Once ruled by the Nizams of Hyderabad—whose jewels are the envy of every museum in the world, and the last of whom was declared the richest man in the world during the 1950s, the state covers an area of 275,000 sq km (106,180 sq miles). It is bordered on the south by Tamil Nadu, on the west by Karnataka, on the north and northwest by Maharashtra, on the northeast by Madhya Pradesh and Orissa, and on the east by the Bay of Bengal. To the north are mountains: Mahendragiri, the highest peak, rises to 1,500 m (4,921 ft). The mighty Krishna and Godavari rivers that bifurcate India into north and south flow through the state.

It is warm and humid most of the time, but when most of northern India is sweltering in 95 per cent humidity and average temperatures of 40° C (104° F) in the months of June, July and August, cool breezes blow through huge parts of Andhra, and at night you may sometimes even need a blanket to keep yourself warm.

Andhra's main urban tourist attraction is Hyderabad, its capital. It was once India's 'pearl city', dominating the world's gem trade. Its production of delicate silver filigree crafts, which provides employment to thousands of artisans, is the envy of world markets. Also wowing international markets is Hyderabad's *kalamkari* (painted or printed fabric on which the patterns are traced with a pen) work. *Kalamkari* is used on clothing and on decorative items such as wall hangings and lamp shades.

Modern Hyderabad is now competing with Bangalore to become the most modern and progressive city in India, with corporations from across the world making a beeline to set up shop here and invest in biotechnology, pharmaceuticals, business management, banking and other sectors.

This old city with a powerful modern face has played host to dignitaries such as former US president Bill Clinton and Microsoft founder Bill Gates. One of the world's best equipped film studios—Ramoji Film City, spread over 405 hectares (1,000 acres)—is a half-hour ride from Hyderabad. The Hyderabad International Exhibition Centre (HITEX) is the country's most up-to-date and well-equipped exhibition venue for trade-related events.

There are plenty of bars, fast-food joints, pool halls, bowling alleys and clubs to keep tourists entertained. But do not miss out on authentic Hyderabadi cuisine— Mughal delicacies from the north spiced with south Indian flavours. Hyderabadi *biryani*—saffron-scented rice with yoghurt-marinated mutton— is unforgettable. Then there is *bagara baigan*, eggplant cooked with sesame seeds, and *tamatter cut*, a hot and sour tomato chutney best eaten with plain boiled rice. Look for eateries offering these items in the

THIS PAGE: The construction of Golconda Fort allowed its last king to hold back invaders for up to eight months.

OPPOSITE: Kalamkari's use of a pen to trace patterns allows for greater finesse; printing blocks are specially created for Andhra Pradesh's textiles.

THIS PAGE: *Droughts are a feature of life in Andhra Pradesh.*

OPPOSITE: *Periyar Wildlife Sanctuary is one of many recognised reserves in India's south.*

Charminar bazaar area of old Hyderabad, where narrow alleys are crowded with merchants selling the most beautiful assortment of lac bangles.

The capital is in reality the twin cities of Hyderabad and Secunderabad, linked by Hussain Sagar Lake. Places of interest are the Charminar ('Four Pillars', the city's icon), built in 1591, Osmania University, Salar Jung Museum, Mecca Masjid, Birla Mandir Temple and Planetarium, and one of the world's largest free-standing stone Buddha statues, situated right in the middle of the lake.

Also of interest is Nehru Zoological Park, one of the world's finest of such facilities, where the animals reside in large, open enclosures. The zoo also supports one of South Asia's best-managed tiger reserves. The Nagarjunasagar Srisailam Sanctuary, sprawling over an area of 3,568 sq km (1,378 sq miles), is one of the world's best. You may not find these names on an ordinary tourist itinerary, but if you are a wildlife enthusiast and have already visited India's heritage sites, then schedule an exclusive sojourn into these still wonderfully preserved areas and get to know a little more about the country's wild inhabitants.

Among the gems of Andhra Pradesh is a formidable fort called Golconda, a 16th-century structure built by the Qutb Shah kings, which lies in the Abids area of Hyderabad. Golconda was one of the richest diamond mining areas in the world, and it produced the famous Kohinoor and Pitt diamonds. The Kohinoor is now the jewel in the crown of the English monarchy.

serenity and calm

The Bay of Bengal also touches Andhra Pradesh. The bay provides the state with gentle beaches, most of them unfrequented by tourists, and provides the waters for the great port of Visakhapatnam, whose most prominent feature is a huge rock that pokes its powerful snout—known as 'Dolphin's Nose'—defiantly into the waters of the Indian Ocean at a height of 174 m (571 ft). That about sums up India—defiant, beckoning, alluring and mystifying.

...schedule an exclusive sojourn into these still wonderfully preserved areas...

Bangaram Island Resort

Imagine waking up to nothing but the sound of waves, the call of seabirds and endless stretches of sandy beaches and aquamarine seas. Bangaram Island is where this fantasy can become a reality. The jewel in a string of islets in Lakshadweep, it is located some 320 km (200 miles) off the coast of Kerala in southwestern India. With only 36 main islands, the stunning archipelago promises pristine beaches, pure waters and an exclusivity that is rare in this age of modern travel.

Divers cannot get enough of the island's underwater world, and are known to return again and again to explore and further enjoy its magnificence. Romantics rave about the fabulous views—how the sand banks stretch on forever before finally disappearing into the sea, and the way the coral atolls are framed by varying hues of blue and green, their shades changing with the shifting waves and position of the sun.

Lakshadweep itself has an interesting history. It is believed to have been discovered by shipwrecked sailors who were washed ashore during a bad storm in 435 AD. So remote are the islands that if not for those ill-fated sailors, they might have remained unknown. Today, the archipelago is home to only 50,000 people, who make

THIS PAGE (CLOCKWISE FROM TOP): *Bangaram Island offers guests a slice of paradise; lazing on the beach has never been so appealing; colourful marine life inhabit the reefs nearby.*
OPPOSITE: *Clear waters in hues of blue and green stretch as far as the eye can see.*

a living from fishing and coconut cultivation. Lakshadweep has maintained its traditional way of life through the years—a slow pace that nurtures tranquillity.

Bangaram Island Resort upholds this laid-back way of life. The island is populated only by the resort's staff, guests and the occasional visitor from Agatti, where the airport is located. As with the other islands, nature has bestowed many gifts which the resort has put to good use. Guests stay in cosy huts right on the beach, with the sand and sea within easy reach.

Each of the 26 Standard Beach Huts is designed for comfort and relaxation. They are intentionally kept simple and functional, with a ceiling fan, refrigerator and en suite bathroom being the most luxurious items. Guests tend to discover that they do not actually need more than this, as most of their time is spent outdoors, or, should the weather not permit, on their palm-covered verandah, where they can savour an aromatic cup of tea from Kerala. Those who require more space will opt for the Deluxe Beach Huts, which can house four guests each. But with

51 hectares (126 acres) of land on the island, guests will not feel crowded even when the resort is at full occupancy.

Meals, which cover the full range of international cuisines, Indian and local recipes, are served at a quaint hut made entirely of bamboo and huge palm fronds, and supported only by one central pole— guests almost always exclaim at this architectural feat. Expect a 'catch of the day' every day on the restaurant's menu. The chefs can whip up delicious fish dishes by the dozen day after day, combining various

Indian ingredients and spices with local cooking styles honed over the years. Every meal is a gastronomic adventure, but always well-suited to the laid-back beach vibe.

There is no need for an air-conditioned lounge or coffee house here, not when you can let the sea breeze ruffle your hair and caress your face, and the setting sun bathe you in its warm glow. There are few places on earth where sunsets are so spectacular, and when you stay at Bangaram Island Resort, you will be free to enjoy such sunsets every day. The bar, which conveniently sits right on the beach, is where guests can observe the ever-changing kaleidoscope of colours as day turns into night, and the moon and stars take their rightful positions in the darkening sky.

Before night falls, however, there are numerous activities to get into. The resort offers a range of sea sports, including scuba diving, snorkelling, deep-sea fishing and kayaking. For those who have never taken the plunge, diving courses are available, as well as starter dives in the less intimidating lagoon under the care of trained divers. The professional dive centre at the resort also organises trips for experienced divers. They will handle everything from boat rides to equipment hire and licenses for dives at offshore reefs, so that participants can just relax and look forward to the wonders that await them at the reefs.

The deep seas surrounding Bangaram Island are a haven for big-game anglers. Barracuda, yellowfin, travelli and wahoo

THIS PAGE (FROM TOP LEFT): *Sandy paths lead guests around the property; thatched roofs add to the rustic, relaxed feel of the island; the huts are located on the beach, so guests barely have to run to hit the water.*

THIS PAGE (BELOW) AND OPPOSITE: *Cruises by day and night allow guests to see the full spectrum of colours found at and around Bangaram Island.*

are plentiful, and promise a good fight for those who dare to take up the challenge. Local boats manned by experienced crew are available for hire. Serious fishermen are advised to come with their own equipment and be prepared to face some of their most enjoyable experiences at sea, while surrounded by some of the best views they will ever witness.

After a day spent outdoors, it is wonderful to feel the soothing touch of therapists skilled in Ayurvedic treatments on your body. This ancient Indian art of healing believes in the balance of body, mind and spirit to achieve well-being. And where better to enjoy Ayurvedic treatments than at a tranquil resort where you are surrounded by untouched natural beauty? Whether for relaxation or the treatment of ailments, the fully-equipped Ayurvedic Centre offers a wide array of therapies and a group of highly competent staff to make your visit a memorable experience.

PHOTOGRAPHS COURTESY OF BANGARAM ISLAND RESORT.

FACTS

ROOMS	26 Standard Beach Huts • 3 Deluxe Beach Huts
FOOD	international
DRINK	beach bar
FEATURES	Ayurvedic Centre • dive centre • scuba diving • snorkelling • deep-sea fishing • boating • kayaking • island hopping
NEARBY	Agatti
CONTACT	Central Reservations, Casino Hotel, Willingdon Island, Cochin 682003, Kerala • telephone: +91.484.3011 711 • facsimile: +91.484.2668 001 • email: bangaramisland@cghearth.com • website: www.cghearth.com

The Brunton Boatyard Hotel

An intimate ambience, a sense of heritage and colonial charm—these are the qualities frequently cited by guests as the main draws of The Brunton Boatyard Hotel. Situated in the port city of Cochin, the property, which was built on the century-old boatyard of Geo, Brunton and Sons, is a repository of nautical history. From the architecture to the interior design, everything reflects the story of Cochin's spice trade.

The tiled forecourt of The Brunton Boatyard Hotel offers a hint of the way things are done at this property—in grand scale. With its high ceiling, beautiful arches and open sides, the lobby is filled with light and cool sea breezes all day. Huge *punkahs*—fans of Indo-Portuguese origin—sway in lazy unison overhead. Previously powered by people to provide respite from the tropical heat, these have moved with the times and are now driven by electricity.

The Brunton Boatyard Hotel has 22 well-appointed rooms and suites. Each of the rooms—and bathrooms—offers glorious sea

THIS PAGE (FROM TOP): The clean and simple interiors of the suites create a sense of space that is in line with the resort-like feel of the hotel; the pool stands at the former entrance of the old boatyard.

OPPOSITE (FROM LEFT): The high four-poster bed comes with a footstool to help guests up; an antique pool table continues to entertain guests looking for a relaxing way to pass their time.

views. So whether you are tucked into your four-poster bed or soaking in the bathtub, you may catch sight of playful dolphins frolicking in the waters just beyond.

Dining at this hotel is quite an experience. As traders arrived from their various ports of call, they left behind a culinary legacy which has made Kerala's cuisine just that bit more exciting. At History, the hotel's main restaurant, the chefs prepare dishes using recipes from some of the oldest families in Cochin. Guests can expect

mouth-watering selections such as pork vindaloo, mulligatawny, Arabian *pulao* (rice dishes), and desserts from Malabar. Add to these dishes the finest Indian herbs and spices, and it is easy to understand why diners rave about the food at History.

Seated at Armoury, a casual coffee shop and bar, and gazing out at the sea, guests will almost feel themselves transported back in time. The sea breeze still kisses the cheeks and teases their hair, just as it did with seafarers of the past.

Relics located near the hotel will reveal the influences of the different people who once passed through India. Vasco da Gama, the famous explorer, achieved what Christopher Columbus did not: he discovered the all-important sea route to the Indies. His memory lives on in the form of a grave, marked by a plaque and brass rails, as well as artefacts which lie in the vicinity of St Francis Church. A walking tour around The Brunton Boatyard Hotel will unveil more of the very rich history of Cochin.

PHOTOGRAPHS COURTESY OF THE BRUNTON BOATYARD HOTEL.

FACTS		
ROOMS	18 Standard Rooms • 4 Deluxe Suites	
FOOD	History: multi-cuisine	
DRINK	Armoury	
FEATURES	Ayurveda Centre • pool	
NEARBY	Fort Cochin • St Francis Church • Jew Street • Mattancherry Palace Museum • Cochin Club • Old Harbour House • Chinese fishing nets • harbour cruise	
CONTACT	Central Reservations, Casino Hotel, Willingdon Island, Cochin 682003, Kerala • telephone: +91.484.3011 711 • facsimile: +91.484.2668 001 • email: contact@cghearth.com • website: www.cghearth.com	

Casino Hotel

To first-time visitors, Kerala comes as a refreshing surprise. Nowhere else can there be found such a harmonious juxtaposition of the old and new, the traditional and modern. Casino Hotel in Cochin offers a wonderful introduction to this beautiful and seamless mix of opposites.

Located on Willingdon Island, a bustling island which was one of the centres of trade during the British Raj, Casino Hotel welcomes every visitor with the age-old Indian greeting of 'varvelpu'. The aarti or garland of fragrant jasmine flowers is presented, followed by some refreshing coconut water. Also emblematic of India through the ages is the genuine warmth and hospitality shown to guests at the hotel, each of whom is treated like a VIP.

THIS PAGE: The ambience complements the mouth-watering seafood perfectly at Fort Cochin.

OPPOSITE: Casino Hotel's dark wood furnishings blend seamlessly with its clean lines and muted lighting.

Fort Cochin...is renowned for its fresh catches and ingenious cooking styles.

The décor at Casino Hotel is the finest mix of the old and new. Gleaming parquet floors, simple elegant lines and modern furnishings complement each other in the luxury rooms and suites. Because of the hotel's strategic location, every room offers unparalleled views of the magnificent waters surrounding the property.

Mealtimes are a special treat at Casino Hotel, especially for those addicted to seafood. Fort Cochin, the speciality seafood restaurant, is renowned for its fresh catches and ingenious cooking styles. Whether it is a serving of prawns, lobsters, salmon or squid, every item is carefully cooked with the finest Indian spices to unlock its special flavours. As the restaurant is packed with gourmands every evening, reservations are highly recommended. Finish off a perfect evening with a cocktail at Vasco da Gama Lounge. Guests who crave food from home will find themselves satisfied at Tharavadu, with its international menu.

Casino Hotel's Cascade Pool is extremely popular with water-lovers. There is no better way to relax than by allowing the falling waters to wash away the tension in the body—or is there? The Ayurveda Centre has a host of therapies to help your body, mind and soul achieve balance.

A diverse mix of activities can be enjoyed in the vicinity of the hotel, ranging from clubbing to shopping, and from history to culture. Ernakulam beckons with shops touting global brands and brightly coloured Indian *saris* and *mundus*—traditional Indian apparel. The old quarters offer eight centuries of heritage from different peoples and religions—Dutch, Portuguese, British, Indian and Chinese, Catholic, Hindu and Jewish. With a wealth of artefacts, tombs, places of worship, residences and more, the old quarters are a haven for history buffs.

PHOTOGRAPHS COURTESY OF CASINO HOTEL.

FACTS		
	ROOMS	66 Standard Rooms • 1 Suite
	FOOD	Tharavadu: international • Fort Cochin: seafood
	DRINK	Vasco da Gama Lounge
	FEATURES	Ayurveda Centre • pool
	BUSINESS	conference centre • banquet facilities
	NEARBY	Dutch Harbour House • Jewish Synagogue • St Francis Church • Cochin Club • Mattancherry Palace • Vasco da Gama's grave • Chinese fishing nets • shopping • harbour cruises
	CONTACT	Central Reservations, Casino Hotel, Willingdon Island, Cochin 682003, Kerala • telephone: +91.484.3011 711 • facsimile: +91.484.2668 001 • email: contact@cghearth.com • website: www.cghearth.com

Coconut Lagoon

Authenticity is what Coconut Lagoon can lay claim to. Everything about this resort is a product of nature, including the ambience which is strictly Keralan in inspiration. Coconut Lagoon lies beside the wide expanse of Vembanad Lake. A quiet serenity perpetually envelops the property, despite nature and all its sights and sounds being so close at hand.

The 1860 mansion which houses the reception area and lobby was brought over in its entirety from the nearby village of Vaikom in 1993. The brass details on the doors and fretted woodwork on the ceilings are reminders of a long-gone age, but still greatly admired today.

Though the resort's accommodations are more contemporary, they reflect the same attention to detail, making each unit distinctive. It may be a trellis pattern, or a row of brass knobs, but no matter how small or intricate the detail, it is features such as these which ensure that no two units are ever exactly the same.

Guests may choose from bungalows, mansions and pool villas for their stay at Coconut Lagoon. Couples who want some privacy usually head for the cottage-style Heritage Bungalows which dot the banks of the lake. The more spacious two-storey Heritage Mansions offer unobstructed views

THIS PAGE (FROM TOP): The pool lies within a coconut grove; the Pool Villa allows guests to enjoy their holiday in utter seclusion.

OPPOSITE: Like all the units at Coconut Lagoon, the mansions feature a mix of contemporary and traditional décor.

of the lake, while the Pool Villas have their own plunge pools. The mansions and villas are particularly well suited to families and small groups of friends. A unique feature of each unit is the open-air bathroom, where guests can feel the warm glow of the sun or gaze up at the twinkling stars at night while soaking in the tub.

Highly recommended for a lazy evening is the sunset cruise onboard a restored rice boat, called a *kettuvallam*. While the boat bobs gently across the lake to the accompaniment of a flute, guests can witness one of Kerala's stunning sunsets.

After the cruise, what better way is there to end the day than at the resort's celebrated Fort Cochin restaurant? At this speciality seafood restaurant, Chef Raju whips up the best from Kerala's waters, whether it is shellfish, squid or just a humble river fish. The mouth-watering aroma of curry, cinnamon, basil and the hundreds of spices that India is renowned for will fill the air, adding to this authentic experience of Keralan cuisine. Most of the ingredients are local, including the red rice which is grown at Coconut Lagoon's own paddy fields. As some guests tend to overindulge, the resort has a menu of Ayurvedic drinks to hopefully soothe stomachs which have been pushed too far.

A stay at Coconut Lagoon is all about unwinding and enjoying a relaxed pace of life, one where guests never feel the need to do anything more than what they want. Sit by the pool, lie in a hammock, go fishing, explore the sights, or just stay in bed all day; it is completely up to you.

PHOTOGRAPHS COURTESY OF COCONUT LAGOON.

FACTS	
ROOMS	28 Heritage Bungalows • 14 Heritage Mansions • 8 Pool Villas
FOOD	Fort Cochin: Keralan, seafood and Ayurvedic drinks
FEATURES	Ayurvedic Centre • pool • recreation centre • library • canoeing • water-skiing • cooking classes • fishing • sunset cruise • backwater cruise
NEARBY	Kumarakom Bird Sanctuary • farm tours
CONTACT	Central Reservations, Casino Hotel, Willingdon Island, Cochin 682003, Kerala • telephone: +91.484.3011 711 • facsimile: +91.484.2668 001 • email: contact@cghearth.com • website: www.cghearth.com

Hotel de L'Orient

Pondicherry, fondly called Pondy, is a quaint coastal town south of Chennai. Once the capital of the French colony, Pondy's colonial heritage is still visible in the broad, straight tree-lined boulevards, bold blooms of bougainvillea, buildings of distinctive cream and yellow, or pink and grey, and its many French monuments, including a miniature Arc de Triomphe, and statues of Joan of Arc and Joseph Françoise Dupleix, the French governor of India.

Set amidst the attractive French part of town is the striking Hotel de L'Orient. Built in the 18th century and substantially restored in the 1990s, it sits just off the main thoroughfare of the central promenade.

Much credit for restoring the property's original neoclassical façade and pink external colour must go to the Neemrana Group, who spent 14 months stripping off years of deterioration and refurbishing the building to match its glory days of the 1880s. Public areas showcase antique lamps, fans, wall hangings, etchings and lithographs from that period.

Today, Hotel de L'Orient is once again a stunning example of French colonial architecture. A key feature of the hotel is its sense of space. High ceilings, elegant arches and a brick-lined garden court ensure that guests feel the warm conviviality of the Orient.

Sixteen rooms are located in the original mansion, set around a shaded central courtyard. The French theme extends to the rooms. Double-beds with coloured glass panels and tiles at the headboards, cane-bottomed reclining chairs, lovely side tables and large wardrobes are a feature of each room. Colourful fabrics offset white walls, creating a distinctly colonial look. Artefacts and wall hangings are also expressive of another era.

Meals are served in the courtyard of the hotel. Dining under the stars can be a particularly memorable experience. Guests are seated inside or under the neem tree in the mansion courtyard where the rooms are, almost as if they are dining below the windows of a residence. The talented chefs will tell you that the food is French Creole, or a mix of two very different cuisines; but whether it is French-, Tamil- or north Indian-inspired, each meal promises to be a treat for the palate, leaving you wanting more.

Those who appreciate heritage and culture will return to Hotel de L'Orient again and again. Not only is it a repository of *objets d'art*, it is also surrounded by buildings of historical significance, all of which will ensure you extend your stay in Pondy, just so you can take in all the sights.

THIS PAGE: *Pondicherry is known for its mix of the French and the Tamil, which leads to interesting, eclectic interiors.*

OPPOSITE (FROM TOP): *The pink façade of the hotel is evocative of its colonial past; the original beauty of the high ceilings, arches and tiles have been carefully restored.*

PHOTOGRAPHS COURTESY OF HOTEL DE L'ORIENT.

FACTS

ROOMS	16 rooms
FOOD	Creole, French, Tamil and north Indian
FEATURES	Neemrana Shop
NEARBY	Gingy Fort • Auroville • Matri Mandir • Sacred Heart Church • Sri Aurobindo Ashram • Gangaikondacholapuram and Chidambaram excursions • heritage walks • boating • campfires • sightseeing • trekking • cruises
CONTACT	17 Rue Romain Rolland, Pondicherry 605001 • telephone: +91.413.2343 067 • facsimile: +91.413.2227 829 • email: sales@neemranahotels.com • website: www.neemranahotels.com

The Leela, Kovalam Beach

There are many reasons why The Leela, Kovalam Beach is one of the top beachfront resorts in Kovalam and its vicinity. The resort has an expansive 1.5 km (0.9 miles) of exclusive beaches, and offers guests every comfort and luxury they desire.

Located just a short distance from Thiruvananthapuram Airport, holidaymakers know that their limited time off will not be wasted on long road trips. As it is perched on a cliff, The Leela offers stunning views of the famed Kovalam coastline and the coconut plantations around it. The vista is especially breathtaking when bathed in the fiery reds and oranges of the setting sun. Coupled with the dance of the waves as the tides change, it is, indeed, a splendid picture of nature at its absolute finest.

The Leela has the honour of being Kerala's first and largest beach resort, and is a favourite with local and foreign visitors alike. But those who have not been at the resort recently are in for a big surprise—The Leela has recently undergone an extensive renovation and upgrading programme to offer guests even more in services and amenities, and the accommodation options look even more appealing now with their ethnic Kerala interior design, vibrant use of colour and contemporary feel. The beach resort ambience, however, has not been lost.

With 194 guestrooms and suites perched on a rock-face on both sides of sweeping beaches, it is no wonder that guests tend to feel that they have arrived at a private beach paradise. With brilliant sunshine day after day, large stretches of clear waters, warm golden sands and unlimited hours to do whatever they desire, it is normal for guests to feel a great reluctance to leave when their holidays come to an end.

Those who are there solely for the beach usually request a room in the resort's largest wing, the Beach-View Wing. Every room here offers views of the shimmering Arabian Sea and the famed Kovalam coast. Just imagine waking up to the mesmerising sight of sun, sea and sand, heralding another day of fun with no meetings to attend and no deadlines to meet. An infinity-edged swimming pool with ocean views is a new addition to this wing, as is the stylish lobby. After breakfast, take a stroll down to the pool or the beach, where you will not have to fight with a dozen other people for a choice spot to lay down your blanket and soak in the peace and tranquillity. The large stretch of beach ensures guests never feel it is crowded.

Each room is attractively styled with a pleasing mix of contemporary and ethnic Kerala designs and colours. Comfortable king-size beds sport bedlinens in vibrant shades, with throw cushions covered in gorgeous silks and satins. Floral motifs feature on the walls, with authentic paintings and photographs. Soft lights illuminate the rich, dark wood panelling commonly found in local architecture. Even though window shades are provided, few guests close them

as this would deprive them of the fabulous views just outside the windows.

Besides the popular Beach-View Wing, there are also the Sea-View and Pavilion Wings. The former is where The Club at The Leela—the hotel's exclusive wing—is located. The Sea-View Wing houses 60 impressive Club Rooms, three Club Suites and the luxurious Maharaja Suite. Among the facilities Club guests can make use of are the Club Lounge and Library, a fine dining restaurant, a wide sea-view terrace and a fully-equipped state-of-the-art spa. Another benefit is The Club's private express check-in/check-out services. With all this and more, guests at The Club can look forward to nothing less than the best and a completely hassle-free holiday.

The Pavilion Wing, with individual parlour rooms, is located on the ground floor, and offers guests sea and garden views.

A holiday is incomplete without experiencing a sensuous, professional massage. The Leela's signature Ayurveda and Wellnesss Spa—offering the best of ancient remedies for rejuvenation and well being—has seven treatment rooms and a dedicated foot massage pavilion. The spa menu is extensive in order to meet the diverse needs of the resort's guests, from stress relief to cures for persistent ailments, or just aching muscles. The therapies offered

work best when complemented by yoga and meditation, and The Leela has large and airy yoga rooms for those who need the space, or enjoy organised group classes. As these rooms offer immediate access to the beach, guests can make the most of the open spaces and natural breeze to enhance their feeling of wellness.

The restaurants at The Leela are legendary for their creativity, sumptuous cuisine, fresh ingredients and constant innovation. The Café, The Tides and The Beach Restaurant are popular, so reservations are highly recommended. Lighter fare and beverages are served at the Pool Lounge.

THIS PAGE: The stunning décor in each room is matched only by the magnificent view of swaying coconut trees and inviting beaches.

OPPOSITE (FROM TOP): Contemporary details prevail in the rooms; with superb food and a beachfront setting, dinner is a mesmerising experience.

FACTS

ROOMS	70 Beach-View Superior Rooms • 16 Beach-View Deluxe Rooms • 2 Beach-View Deluxe Suites • 20 Garden-View Pavilion Rooms • 22 Sea-View Pavilion Rooms • 60 Sea-View Club Rooms • 3 Club Suites • 1 Maharaja Suite
FOOD	The Café: international and Indian • The Beach Restaurant: international
DRINK	The Bar • Pool Lounge
FEATURES	Ayurveda Wellness Spa • pool • fitness centre • jogging track • water sports
BUSINESS	Internet access • conference centre • secretarial services • business centre
NEARBY	Veli Tourist Village • The Napier Museum • backwater cruises • plantation visits
CONTACT	Trivandrum 695527, Kerala • telephone: +91.471.2480 101 • facsimile: +91.471.2481 522 • email: reservations.kovalam@theleela.com • website: www.theleela.com

PHOTOGRAPHS COURTESY OF THE LEELA, KOVALAM BEACH.

The Leela Palace Kempinski, Bangalore

The Leela Palace Kempinski, Bangalore is an unexpected surprise for travellers more accustomed to the contemporary designs of most city hotels. Stately and grand, this six-storey hotel draws its inspiration from the famous Royal Palace of Mysore, ancient forts of the Vijayanagar Empire, and temples of a bygone era. The magnificent façade of The Leela Palace Kempinski—with its high arches, copper domes and regal bearing— is a good indication of the splendour that lies within. Its location is also ideal. Sited midway between the international airport and the city centre, it offers the optimal balance of convenience and flexibility.

Thick hand-knotted carpets in rich hues cover the hardwood floors, and only the best crystals and finest bone china are used. Dark wood, plush furniture, ornate curves and smooth lines offer stylish touches. Whichever way you turn, the décor is soothing and the ambience tranquil.

Since its opening, the hotel has been the talk of the town for its design and dining concepts, and service standards. In fact, it won its first international award from *Forbes* magazine within a year of opening, when it made the coveted list of 'Best New Business Hotels of 2001'. More than 2,300 sq m (24,760 sq ft) of dedicated meeting facilities on one floor, superb banquet and guest services, numerous conference spaces

and the largest column-free grand ballroom in Bangalore make it a natural inclusion in the *Forbes* list.

Overseas meetings and conventions are a common sight at the hotel, with organisers citing its unique blend of state-of-the-art amenities, world-class service and heritage architecture raising it a cut above the rest.

Every one of the well-appointed guestrooms has a private balcony with an unrivalled view of the shimmering pool or

verdant gardens. In-room high-speed Internet access, a large work table, concierge service and a butler on call round-the-clock are among the many service initiatives put in place to pamper guests.

The Royal Club—located on the two top floors of the hotel—is a particular favourite of business travellers who want additional privacy and personalised attention. There are 53 rooms, six Executive Suites and the Maharaja Suite at the Royal Club. Exclusively for Royal Club guests are the Champagne Lounge, Billiards/Sports Lounge and Cigar Lounge, ideal spaces for relaxation, small meetings and networking.

The two signature restaurants at The Leela rank among the best in Bangalore, with a high percentage of walk-in and regular guests. Often seen enjoying the delectable cuisine are the who's who of India, foreign dignitaries and food and wine connoisseurs seeking the finer things in life.

THIS PAGE (FROM TOP):
Inspiring, elegant and stately, The Leela Palace Kempinski is a welcome haven from the constant buzz of the city; a curved staircase overlooks the grounds of the hotel.
OPPOSITE: The hotel's design reflects the rich architectural style of the Royal Palace of Mysore.

THIS PAGE: Take a dip in the pool, relax in the jacuzzi or soak up the sun on a poolside deck chair.

OPPOSITE (FROM TOP): Floor-to-ceiling windows invite guests to bask in natural light and enjoy the beautiful landscape outside; the regal and luxuriously appointed Maharaja Suite has welcomed royalty from many countries.

Drawing from over 600 years of tradition, Jamavar, the Indian speciality restaurant, offers dishes from north and south India. In a dining area reminiscent of a palace, the chefs present a menu which initiates, titillates and then satiates diners in search of superlative Indian cuisine.

Zen, with its fusion of modern and traditional Indian design, serves up a storm with the varied cuisines of Asia: Japanese, Thai, Indonesian, Malay and more are on the extensive menu. For those who have more unconventional meal times or would like some food from home, Citrus, the 24-hour brasserie, serves international food. Its selection of mouth-watering pizzas served fresh from wood-fired ovens is especially popular with diners.

The Library Bar certainly lives up to its scholarly name with its dark wood panels, comfortable settees, soft lighting and a long list of drinks. There is really no better place to unwind after a day spent exploring the sights of Bangalore.

Guests who love retail therapy will not want to miss The Leela Galleria, the city's

sq m (20,000 sq ft). Its plethora of traditional and modern treatments are a hit particularly with the city's stressed IT professionals.

More active guests will appreciate the many programmes available at the fitness centre. From one-to-one workouts with certified trainers to group sessions of yoga, aerobics and kick-boxing, there is a schedule to meet every guest's needs.

Bangalore has much to offer visitors with time to spare. Historical and cultural sites, lovely gardens and parks, and the KGA Golf Club are easily accessible from The Leela Palace Kempinski.

largest shopping centre. Expect a shop-till-you-drop experience—many guests have commented that a full day is not enough to enjoy the wonderful array of fine wares and souvenirs available. Another attraction here is the 24-hour nightclub.

After all that shopping and dancing, guests of The Leela Palace Kempinski know exactly where to go to relax—The Spa. Bangalore's largest urban spa is spread over three levels and occupies at least 1,858

FACTS		
ROOMS	100 Deluxe Rooms • 49 Conservatory Rooms • 28 Conservatory Premiere Rooms • 57 Royal Club Rooms • 5 Royal Club Suites • 7 Turret Suites • 7 Executive Suites • 2 Deluxe Suites • 1 Maharaja Suite
FOOD	Jamavar: Indian • Zen: Asian • Citrus: international
DRINK	Library Bar
FEATURES	The Spa • The Leela Galleria shopping mall • pool • gym
BUSINESS	Internet access • business centre • boardrooms and meeting rooms
NEARBY	Krishna Raja Sagar Dam • Brindavan Gardens • Tipu's Fort
CONTACT	23 Airport Road, Bangalore 560008, Karnataka • telephone: +91.80.2521 1234 • facsimile: +91.80.2521 2222 • email: reservations@theleelablr.com • website: www.theleela.com

PHOTOGRAPHS COURTESY OF THE LEELA PALACE KEMPINSKI, BANGALORE.

Malabar House

Malabar House, located in the vibrant port city of Cochin, has been sensitively restored and looks every bit the pretty Dutch colonial villa that it once was. This, coupled with the hospitality of its well-trained staff, makes guests feel as if they have taken a step back in time to an era of elegance and high tea in the tropics.

Malabar House has 17 luxury rooms and suites, all of which are decked out in a lively mix of contemporary and antique furnishings. Bold colours meet subdued hues, and strong lines are softened by artful lighting. The result is an ambience which is soothing, comfortable and luxurious.

The Malabar Suite is a duplex measuring a generous 50 sq m (538 sq ft). It comes with its own private roof garden terrace, which is ideal for small gatherings or for relaxing with a good book and some chilled wine. There are a further five suites with roof gardens for those who do not require so much space, but appreciate the exclusivity. Capitalising on the boutique hotel's picturesque surroundings, the Deluxe Rooms all come with private gardens.

THIS PAGE (CLOCKWISE FROM TOP): A unique swing-bed takes pride of place on a verandah; the pool is set in a pleasant courtyard; rooms are adorned with a pleasing mix of old and new.

OPPOSITE (FROM LEFT): Malabar Junction serves a sumptuous mix of cuisines; the Malabar Suite offers families and small groups more space to unwind.

...looks every bit the pretty Dutch colonial villa that it once was.

Seafood-lovers are in for a treat. Malabar Junction, the hotel's speciality seafood restaurant, is renowned for its succulent and fresh catches. Mediterranean and Indian fare are also served here, and guests are always eager to tuck into these dishes, especially upon catching the unmistakable and tantalising aroma of spicy Indian cuisine in the air. You are bound to leave with a satisfied stomach.

Many people have heard of the ancient therapies of Ayurveda, but not specifically of *kalari*—an age-old treatment that mixes Ayurvedic-based herbal treatments with a massage regimen which aims to repair physiological damage. Malabar House's Ayurvedic Kalari Spa offers soothing, rejuvenating treatments based on the *kalari* school. Guests with specific ailments can opt for sustained *kalari* treatments spanning three days to a fortnight.

Malabar House is surrounded by monuments of great historical significance. Jew Town is a living heritage centre, and visitors often stop by the synagogue to explore the centuries-old but still functioning place of worship. Street vendors liven up the area with a showcase of multi-coloured masks, antique lamps and souvenirs of all kinds. Also nearby are St Francis Church and Vasco da Gama's tomb. Guests should set aside at least four days to fully soak in the rich history and culture of this area.

FACTS		
ROOMS	11 Deluxe Rooms • 5 Roof Garden Suites • 1 Malabar Suite	
FOOD	Malabar Junction: seafood, Indian and Mediterranean	
FEATURES	Ayurvedic Kalari Spa • pool	
BUSINESS	conference and exhibition hall	
NEARBY	St Francis Church • Jew Town • Vasco da Gama's tomb • Chinese fishing nets • backwater cruises • walking tours • fish market	
CONTACT	1/268 + 1/269 Parade Road, Fort Cochin, Kochi 682001, Kerala • telephone: +91.484.2216 666 • facsimile: +91.484.2217 777 • email: info@malabarhouse.com • website: www.malabarhouse.com	

PHOTOGRAPHS COURTESY OF MALABAR HOUSE.

Marari Beach Resort

Imagine a beach where the only sounds you will hear are birdcalls and the waves, where golden sands gleam in welcome, where no pedlars disturb your peace nor joggers kick sand over you. This is what you will find at the serene and pristine beach paradise known as Marari Beach Resort.

Located in a small village in Mararikulam, this spacious 52-room resort is designed to blend completely into the traditional Indian way of life. With the Arabian Sea and unspoilt beaches right at its doorstep, guests can forget all their worries and enjoy a truly relaxing time.

Along with peace and quiet, giving guests more personal space is yet another aim of the resort, with each villa separated from the next by generous stretches of lush greenery. Pathways meander through the vegetation, linking each villa to the common areas. Lotus ponds with vibrant blooms, ancient stone walls hugged by creepers and flowers, and large trees with wide branches all add to the secluded atmosphere and languid pace of life.

The Garden Villa is built to resemble a local fisherman's hut. With its thatched palm-leaf roof sloping to meet the raised

verandah, guests are easily misled into thinking that the interior is equally rustic and natural, which it is not. Each villa is simply but elegantly furnished, with modern amenities and an interesting—albeit traditional—open-air bathroom in an enclosed, private courtyard. The Pool Villa, as its name suggests, comes with its own pool and living room.

Seafood is the outstanding highlight of every meal at Marari Beach Resort. Expect fresh prawns, lobsters, fish and more when you dine at Fort Cochin. The talented chefs can whip up the most tantalising dishes, complemented by the herbs and spices that Kerala is recognised for. After dinner, head to the Beach Shack and Bar. Here, amidst the sound of breaking waves as night falls, you can enjoy a chat with your loved ones while sipping on an ice-cold drink.

During the day, there are a number of recreational activities to keep guests occupied, should they feel the need to do something other than lie on the beach. Cycle through the village, sign up for a cooking class, or just head to the Ayurveda Centre and indulge in a healing treatment. The centre also conducts yoga classes.

Whatever you choose, you can be sure that at Marari Beach Resort, your holiday will be as active or relaxing as you want it to be.

THIS PAGE: *Al fresco dining in the lush gardens of the resort is an unforgettable experience.*

OPPOSITE (FROM TOP): *With its predominant use of palm leaves and thatch, each villa resembles a traditional fisherman's hut; the generous open spaces and lotus ponds enhance the feeling of peace and serenity.*

PHOTOGRAPHS COURTESY OF MARARI BEACH RESORT.

FACTS		
ROOMS	49 Garden Villas • 10 Garden Pool Villas • 3 Deluxe Pool Villas	
FOOD	Fort Cochin: international, Keralan and seafood • Beach Shack: seafood and buffet	
DRINK	Club House Bar • Beach Bar	
FEATURES	Ayurveda Centre • pool • tennis • yoga • cooking classes • library • cycling • indoor games	
NEARBY	fishing villages • shops	
CONTACT	Central Reservations, Casino Hotel, Willingdon Island, Cochin 682003, Kerala • telephone: +91.484.3011 711 • facsimile: +91.484.2668 001 • email: contact@cghearth.com • website: www.cghearth.com	

The Oberoi, Bangalore

Bangalore is the capital of Karnataka state. It is a city which is home to cutting-edge research and a flourishing electronics industry. Visitors are apt to imagine a city filled with commercial buildings, offices and manufacturing facilities. This is why the wonderful expanse of parks, wide tree-lined boulevards and stately buildings come as a pleasant surprise to first-time visitors. Located 1,000 m (3,281 ft) above sea level, Bangalore enjoys lovely weather all year.

The Oberoi, Bangalore mirrors the city's park-like atmosphere with its own verdant grounds, creating the perfect haven for guests seeking a serene place to call home. As such, business travellers are well cared for at The Oberoi. The hotel's Deluxe Rooms come with an in-room fax machine, wireless Internet access, voice mail and a dual-line telephone. A 24-hour, state-of-the-art business centre, two conference halls equipped with satellite teleconferencing facilities and excellent banquet venues complete the hotel's business travel experience. All the Deluxe Rooms and Suites enjoy round-the-clock butler service.

The spacious Presidential Suite is the accommodation of choice for VIPs and senior management. With a sauna, pantry, separate living and dining areas, a private terrace and two-poster bed, the suite is designed for luxury, comfort and exclusivity.

Whether it is golf or squash, historical landmarks or shrines, everything is at your fingertips.

Wining and dining is always a pleasure at The Oberoi. And there is no better way to begin the experience than with a drink at The Polo Club. Recalling the days when polo games were all the rage in India, this popular bar—offering superb views of the hotel's gardens—has wall hangings featuring the game in play, and wickerwork chairs that hint at an elegant colonial past. When it is time to head to dinner, choose from Continental and Indian cuisine at Le Jardin, Szechwan and other Chinese specialities at The Szechwan Court, or Thai food at Rim Nam, an al fresco restaurant set by a picturesque pond.

The Oberoi is well regarded for its conservation efforts. Not only does it pay great attention to energy conservation, it also strives to minimise environmental pollution in everything it does.

Guests who stroll through the manicured gardens often stop to marvel at the famous 75-year-old rain tree, which embodies the 'green spirit' of the hotel. Rather than destroying it, The Oberoi was built around it, respecting its place in nature.

Guests also have the option of visiting The Oberoi Spa and Fitness Centre by Banyan Tree. The Oberoi, Bangalore is located in a recreational and heritage hub. Whether it is golf or squash, historical landmarks or shrines, everything is at your fingertips. Just ask your butler for directions.

FACTS

ROOMS	121 Premium Rooms • 30 Deluxe Rooms • 4 Executive Suites • 4 Deluxe Suites • 1 Presidential Suite
FOOD	Le Jardin: Indian and Continental • Rim Nam: Thai • The Szechwan Court: Szechwan and Chinese
FEATURES	The Oberoi Spa and Fitness Centre by Banyan Tree • pool • book and souvenir shop • beauty salon • barber shop • travel desk
BUSINESS	business centre • conference rooms
NEARBY	Vidhana Soudha • Tipu Sultan's summer palace • shopping • nature parks
CONTACT	39 Mahatma Gandhi Road, Bangalore 560001, Karnataka • telephone: +91.80.2558 5858 • facsimile: +91.80.2558 5960 • email: reservations@oberoiblr.com • website: www.oberoihotels.com

PHOTOGRAPHS COURTESY OF THE OBEROI, BANGALORE.

The Oberoi, Motor Vessel Vrinda, Backwaters of Kerala

Kerala, commonly known as 'God's own country', is one of India's best kept secrets. Speak to anyone who has visited this coastal region in the southwest, and they will sing its praises. In particular, they will rave about the picturesque backwaters unique to Kerala.

The Oberoi, Motor Vessel Vrinda, a luxury craft, is the best way to explore these backwaters. Comprising a network of lakes, canals, estuaries and deltas, the backwaters support a self-sustaining ecosystem, and are a lifeline of the coastal villages.

The Vrinda is an exclusive craft designed for comfortable sightseeing on the

THIS PAGE (FROM TOP): The restaurant provides an unobstructed view of Kerala's serene backwaters; being onboard the Vrinda is a great way to explore the multiple, meandering waterways of the state.

OPPOSITE: Each cabin is beautifully styled, offering facilities and amenities comparable to top hotels.

water. It has eight beautifully styled Luxury Cabins, all on the lower deck. Like a well-appointed hotel room, each cabin is air-conditioned, and comes with an en suite bathroom, king-size bed, television and DVD player, and an electronic safe. The wooden floors and dark wood furniture lend a stately elegance to the cabins, while the large windows offer an unobstructed view of the backwaters and coastal vegetation.

Breakfast is served in the restaurant on the upper deck. Early risers are promised a spectacular kaleidoscope of colour as the sun begins its daily ascent. Sunset promises an equally memorable display.

Guests on-board the Vrinda have an extensive menu of international and regional cuisines to choose from. Located on the upper deck, the dining room offers guests a 360-degree view of the surroundings through large picture windows. After-dinner cocktails are served at the lounge and bar.

...a 360-degree view of the surroundings through large picture windows.

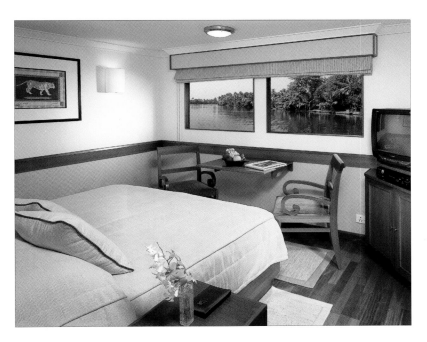

The well-prepared four-night/five-day itinerary comprises one night in Cochin, and three nights on the Vrinda, combining a traditional land tour and hotel stay with a unique on-board experience.

The four-day Vrinda cruise brings guests across Vembanad Lake, the largest stretch of the backwaters. Surrounded by serene waters, the slow, scenic tour is an ideal time to take things easy, savour the peace and quiet, and enjoy the view. In the evening, guests will take in a traditional *kathakali* dance performance on-board the Vrinda.

The Vrinda will then sail south to Alleppey, passing one of the few areas in the world where farming is done below sea level. At Kanjippadam, guests will transfer to a smaller, traditional rice boat, which will meander down the narrow waterways, showcasing a way of life unique to the region. Stops will be made to visit the statue of Buddha at Karumadi, and a Keralan *tharavad* (family residence).

On day three, the Vrinda will head for Chambakulam, where guests will visit a historical church and temple. A highlight is the *mohiniattam* performance on-board the vessel in the evening. This classical dance, distinctive to Kerala, will introduce guests to a slow, graceful style of dance made more intriguing by its traditional costumes.

On day four, guests will be brought to Cochin for a night in a luxury hotel.

FACTS		
ROOMS	8 Luxury Cabins	
FOOD	international and regional	
DRINK	lounge • bar	
FEATURES	sun deck • restaurant with 360-degree views	
ITINERARY	Vembanad Lake • Allepy Canal • *kathakali* dance • Pamba River • Kanjippadam rice boat tour • Karumadi • traditional Kerala *tharavad* • St Mary's Church • Sree Bhagavathy Kshetram • Chambakulam snake boatyard • *mohiniattam* dance	
CONTACT	Corporate Marketing Division, 7 Sham Nath Marg, New Delhi 110054 • telephone: +91.11.2389 0505 • facsimile: +91.11.2389 0582 • website: www.oberoihotels.com	

PHOTOGRAPHS COURTESY OF THE OBEROI, MOTOR VESSEL VRINDA, BACKWATERS OF KERALA.

The Park, Bangalore

India's first contemporary boutique hotel, The Park, Bangalore continues to garner awards for its elegant design and superb service. Located in an upscale district, where retail, high fashion and executive offices abound, the hotel aims to impress even the most discerning and well-travelled guest with its eye-catching décor.

Designed as the ultimate urban retreat in India's 'Garden City', The Park has a white façade which belies the multitude of colours infusing its interior. From the rich black leather found in the lifts to the bold hues used on each of the hotel's four floors, every vibrant design element blends seamlessly to create a sophisticated, elegant and visually stunning location.

All the rooms and suites follow a chic, minimalist style, and are practical in function. A fascinating mix of colours, textures and materials is used—the softest silks, leather, oak and glass—to create a unique feel, which is both refreshing and relaxing. Guests can choose from a variety of rooms located on four residential floors, each bearing a different theme. The first floor, for example, uses blue as a base colour, signifying water, complemented by orange, signifying the sun. Ambience aside, the 26-cm-thick (10-inch-thick) custom-made

THIS PAGE (FROM TOP): Monsoon's great food and vibrant ambience make for a memorable dining experience; the décor of i-bar is just as captivating as other spaces in the hotel.

OPPOSITE: The use of cream and yellow bedlinen against the dark furnishings of the Premier Suite makes a striking impact.

...a white façade which belies the multitude of colours infusing its interior.

mattress in each room will surely help even an insomniac get a good night's sleep.

Interesting concepts are commonplace at The Park. At Monsoon, the hotel's 24-hour restaurant, diners can choose to sit at the well-appointed eatery or opt for a cosy poolside gazebo. The menu is packed with international specialities spanning favourites from the Mediterranean, Southeast Asia and India, making a dining experience here a guaranteed gourmet's delight.

At i-t.Alia, dark wood floors, black upholstery and lime-green sofas create the ideal setting for a satisfying Italian meal of wood-fired oven pizzas, delicious seafood spreads, pasta and more.

Guests who feel the need to watch their weight while enjoying the delicacies of Monsoon or i-t.Alia will be pleased to know they can work off their meals at Aquazone, the hotel's health and fitness area. Head for the all-season lap pool, or go straight to the fully-equipped gym. Steam and sauna rooms

are available, as is an extensive spa menu offering therapies ranging from traditional Ayurvedic remedies to Western treatments.

With its large presence of high-tech companies, Bangalore has earned a second nickname: 'Silicon Valley of India'. Living up to this moniker is The Park's i-bar, a lounge which positively sizzles with high energy. Comfortable beanbags, low furniture and neon shades dominate, set against a colourful wall carpet woven to resemble a circuit board.

The Park, Bangalore's strategic location allows it to offer not only the best in facilities and services within its premises, but also brings the finest amenities of the city closer to its guests. The hotel is a short distance from the shoppers' paradise marked by Brigade Road, Residency Road, Mahatma Gandhi Road and Commercial Street. Those out for a morning stroll will appreciate the stillness of Cubbon Park and Ulsoor Lake, which begins where The Park ends.

FACTS

ROOMS	36 Deluxe Rooms • 34 Deluxe Rooms with balconies • 6 Deluxe Terrace Rooms • 8 Luxury Rooms • 20 The Residence Rooms • 4 Terrace Suites • 1 Premier Suite
FOOD	Monsoon: international • i-t.Alia: Italian
DRINK	i-bar
FEATURES	Aquazone health spa and fitness centre • all-season pool • The Box • The Blue Box in-house theatre • library • boutique gift shop
BUSINESS	high-speed Internet access • Wi-Fi connectivity
NEARBY	Cubbon Park • Ulsoor Lake • Vidhan Soudha • Bangalore Fort
CONTACT	14/7 Mahatma Gandhi Road, Bangalore 560042, Karnataka • telephone: +91.80.2559 4666 • facsimile: +91.80.2559 4667 • email: resv.blr@theparkhotels.com • website: www.theparkhotels.com

PHOTOGRAPHS COURTESY OF THE PARK, BANGALORE.

The Park, Chennai

The Park, Chennai, located in the business district of Tamil Nadu's capital, promises drama, action and a hip vibe, and delivers more. A luxury hotel built on the premises of the historic Gemini Film Studios, both its public and private spaces pay tribute to the larger-than-life movie icons of the 1940s.

The hotel uses a unique mix of textures, surfaces, shadow and light to create a stunning impact. At night, guests are greeted by an interactive space with lights, sounds and images projected on various surfaces, re-enacting the movie buzz of yesteryear.

Positioned as an upmarket urban haven, every room and suite at The Park is elegantly crafted for a restful and unforgettable stay. Soothing colours, pale beech wood flooring and frosted glass blend perfectly with subtle traditional touches like coconut shell-inlaid tables and parchment lights.

The Residence, The Park's exclusive floor, offers personalised service and is designed for the most discerning travellers. Express check-in/check-out, state-of-the-art boardroom facilities, use of The Residence Lounge, masseur service, and bath menus are just some of the little extras offered by the hotel to its special guests. The interiors are adorned with a premium collection of artworks, wall hangings and artefacts.

THIS PAGE (FROM TOP): Relax at the pool, where cabanas and double beds come draped in flowing fabrics; the Presidential Suite has a smart, contemporary look.

OPPOSITE (FROM TOP): The muted lights, gold accents and décor of the suites induce a sense of calm; the perfect balance of soft fabrics, curved lines and hard finishes is found in all public and private spaces.

Constantly winning rave reviews from satisfied diners is the hotel's restaurant Six-o-One, which is open all day. With visual spectacles including awesome light columns soaring 6 m (20 ft) high, breathtaking 'live' performances by the chefs, and gastronomic delights spanning authentic Italian and international classics, it is little wonder that the restaurant is so popular with locals and visitors alike.

The Leather Bar is unashamedly masculine. The floors are covered in rich black leather, while the walls are olive suede. Inspired by Chennai's standing as the 'City of Leather', the bar features numerous artefacts and books on leather. Come sundown, the DJ uses a fusion of sound and images to fashion the ideal location for partying the night away. The outdoor terrace allows guests to enjoy the cool sea breeze.

Guests who prefer to unwind with a workout can head to the hotel's eighth-floor swimming pool, which offers a magnificent view of the city, while one floor up, a well-equipped fitness centre awaits. The best way to cool off after a strenuous workout is to stop by the spa, where guests can choose from a wealth of treatments.

Ideally located in the centre of Chennai, The Park is within walking distance of many sights of interest, including Valluvar Kottam, a memorial to the poet-saint Tiruvalluvar, and Marina Beach, the second longest beach in the world and home to a lovely lighthouse.

PHOTOGRAPHS COURTESY OF THE PARK, CHENNAI.

FACTS	
ROOMS	149 Deluxe Rooms • 18 Luxury Rooms • 9 Suites • 38 The Residence Rooms
FOOD	Six-o-One: Italian and international • Lotus: Thai • Aqua: poolside café
DRINK	The Leather Bar • Wine Room • Pasha the Nightclub
FEATURES	The Box • The Screening Room • stretch pool • spa • gym and health club • boutique gift shop • indoor games • in-house theatre • women-only floor
BUSINESS	high-speed Internet access • dual-line phones • private dining • conference rooms
NEARBY	San Thome Basilica • Valluvar Kottam • Light House • Fort St George • Marina Beach • Kalpaleshwarar Temple • Spencers Plaza
CONTACT	601 Anna Salai, Chennai 600006, Tamil Nadu • telephone: +91.44.5214 4000 • facsimile: +91.44.5214 4100 • email: resv.che@theparkhotels.com • website: www.theparkhotels.com

Serenity at Kanam Estate

A two-and-a-half-hour drive from Cochin Airport will bring guests to the picturesque 1920s bungalow known as Serenity at Kanam Estate. The property's hilltop location offers an amazing view over the Blue Mountains of the Western Ghats and the surrounding plantations.

The most pleasant surprise for first-time visitors is the air—fresh, crisp and tinged with aromatic smells, which is not surprising as there are many cocoa, coffee and spice plantations nearby, as well as fruit orchards.

Lovingly restored and decorated in a style true to its colonial past, Serenity is a stylish and cosy bungalow. While its façade exhibits the clean lines associated with the architecture of an earlier era, it is the interior which charms the most. Dark wood and panelling are used liberally throughout the property, and these are complemented perfectly by the generous use of colonial and local furnishings.

The boutique hotel has five bedrooms, all of which are designed and equipped to keep guests comfortable. Perhaps the most outstanding feature of the hotel and its rooms is the collection of artefacts and paintings diligently assembled over many years and now on display for all to enjoy.

Guests can acquaint themselves with the history of India by exploring the bungalow and paying close attention to details, from the design elements to the salon-style wooden windows, antique ornaments, wall hangings, coir carpets and locally made cotton linens. The antique gramophone, very much a collector's item today, still plays the owner's personal collection of classical and jazz LPs

THIS PAGE (CLOCKWISE FROM TOP): The restored plantation bungalow uses dark wood and bright hues to perfection; Serenity offers the perfect balance of the old and new, in both architecture and facilities; antique artworks are prominently displayed.
OPPOSITE: The rooms are striking in their simplicity.

to perfection. It is easy to imagine yourself at Serenity some 80 or so years ago, revelling in the company of good friends, sumptuous food and drinks, and listening to music from the same gramophone.

Mealtimes are a special event at Serenity, largely because the resident chef himself is in attendance to take orders and make recommendations before he disappears into the kitchen to whip up a gourmet meal. Indian and Mediterranean specialities are served daily.

As the bungalow is located in a huge compound amidst verdant greens, slow strolls along the footpaths are popular, as are bicycle rides around the plantations. Guests usually also indulge in an Ayurvedic massage at the spa before they check-out.

In the vicinity of Serenity are plantations growing a variety of spices and fruits, numerous villages, ancient churches and temples, and handicraft and cultural centres, all waiting to be explored.

PHOTOGRAPHS COURTESY OF SERENITY AT KANAM ESTATE.

FACTS		
	ROOMS	5 rooms
	FOOD	Indian and Mediterranean
	FEATURES	pool • Ayuverdic treatment spa and gym • mountain biking
	BUSINESS	drawing room
	NEARBY	Aranmula Culture Centre • Ettumanur Shiva Temple • Cherai Palli Church • Valia Palli Church • guided plantation walks • elephant and mahout outing • orchid nurseries • local villages
	CONTACT	Payikad, Kanam PO 686515 Vazhoor, Kerala • telephone: +91.481.2456 353/484.2216 666 • facsimile: +91.481.2456 353 • email: info@malabarhouse.com • website: www.malabarhouse.com

Shalimar Spice Garden Resort

The air is always crisp and fresh at Shalimar Spice Garden Resort, situated some 800 m (2,625 ft) above sea level in the mountains at the fringe of the famous Periyar Tiger Reserve. Located in an area where nature rules and modernisation has yet to arrive in full force, it is no surprise that the resort is home to numerous species of plants and trees along with a host of spices, from which the resort derives its name.

All the necessary elements for an idyllic, back-to-nature getaway are present here—cool air, bubbling streams, abundant greenery, and a great respect for the natural world. There is also a symbolic bridge acting as the resort's link to the outside world. Cross this wooden bridge and guests enter a breathtakingly beautiful sanctuary, where a warm, friendly and all-natural experience awaits.

Take a look at the cottages and rooms, especially their thatched roofs, wooden beams and furnishings, and you will quickly discern the use of numerous materials found locally in Kerala. The resort promotes the use of natural materials and a focus on tradition and authenticity. On the property, guests will find a heritage Keralan home which was

taken apart, transported in pieces to the resort and then re-assembled, complete with its original carved wood panels.

A thick undergrowth of vegetation enhances the privacy of each cottage, where guests can sit on their verandah and take in the sights, sounds and scents of nature. The ambience is one of serenity, interrupted only by birdsong and the buzz of insects.

Dining is a casual affair at Shalimar Spice Garden. Every home-cooked meal is carefully prepared with the finest ingredients from the resort's own farms and plantations.

Between meals, the resort offers several options to while away the hours. Besides exploring the grounds, guests can make use of the library or the pool, which is surrounded by tall trees and framed by the mountains.

The resort's Ayurveda and Yoga Centre has a wide menu of therapies. Treatments are more effective when the pace of life is slow and the environment is conducive to relaxation—which is exactly what Shalimar

Spice Garden Resort offers. The centre's qualified Ayurvedic doctors and highly skilled masseurs can carry out seven- or 14-day programmes involving massage, diet and yoga. These programmes are structured to create a holistic package, in order to achieve balance in the body, mind and soul—the very basis of Ayurveda.

THIS PAGE: Guests by the pool sometimes feel as if they have stumbled upon a secret pond in the middle of a verdant jungle.

OPPOSITE (FROM TOP): Surrounded by thick foliage, the cottages offer complete privacy; guests who cross the wooden bridge enter a haven of peace and quiet.

FACTS		
	ROOMS	5 cottages • 10 rooms
	FOOD	Continental, Indian and Italian
	FEATURES	Ayurveda and Yoga Centre • pool • spice gardens • library
	NEARBY	Periyar Wildlife Sanctuary • plantations
	CONTACT	Murikkady PO Kumily 685535, District Idukki, Kerala • telephone: +91.4869.222 132 • facsimile: +91.4869.223 022 • email: shalimar_resort@vsnl.com • website: www.shalimarkerala.com

PHOTOGRAPHS COURTESY OF SHALIMAR SPICE GARDEN RESORT.

Shreyas Retreat

One hour away from the buzz of Bangalore city is a secluded boutique retreat located amidst more than 10 hectares (25 acres) of serene gardens, rice fields and a coconut plantation.

The Vedic instruction, *atithi devo bhava*, 'treat thy guest as an embodiment of the Divine', is the guiding principle behind Shreyas Retreat's excellent service attitude. But its exclusivity—it caters to a maximum of 25 guests at full occupancy, tranquillity and holistic approach to wellness are what keep guests returning again and again.

Shreyas Retreat is dedicated to helping visitors achieve a perfect balance in body, mind and spirit. In Indian custom, 'shreyas' refers to 'all-round excellence', an axiom the retreat aims to fulfil with each of its guests. From its calming façade to the cuisine, yoga classes, spa menus and no-alcohol policy,

THIS PAGE: Shreyas Retreat complements its natural surroundings with the extensive use of natural materials.

OPPOSITE: A direct path leads from a cottage to a private sun deck and swimming pool.

every detail is carefully considered so that guests are provided with optimal opportunities to realise material and mental harmony, however short their stay.

Being a boutique spa retreat, Shreyas has only 12 units for accommodation, comprising eight luxurious tents and four pool cottages. Because the number of guests is low and staff go about their jobs so unobtrusively, the feeling of arriving at your own private sanctuary comes easily.

Each well-appointed tent sits on its own plot of land, surrounded by a generous expanse of trees and vegetation. Wake up every morning to the welcoming sounds of nature, throw open the windows and doors, stretch languorously, and inhale deeply. Let the crisp air replace the smog from the city, and feel your senses come to life as you soak in the beauty of your surroundings.

Belying the idea that tent living means roughing it out, every tent at Shreyas Retreat is built for comfort. En suite bathrooms open onto private walled courtyards, and exquisite patchwork quilts add a homey touch, keeping guests snug at night. Broadband Internet access is available in every unit for those who really cannot let go of the outside world.

The cottages are just as exclusive. Each one is conceptualised to soothe, restore and rejuvenate. The three cottages surround a

...takes guests away from the stresses of life and puts them on the path towards rejuvenation.

THIS PAGE: *The clear night sky, calm waters and twinkling lights create the perfect setting for a private dinner by the pool.*

OPPOSITE (FROM TOP): *The bright and airy living room of the cottage features contemporary design, with artefacts and wall hangings of Indian origin; the Yoga Hall is well-suited not only for yoga, but meditation as well.*

central pool, and the single three-bedroom cottage, ideal for families or small groups, comes with its own living room. The deck chairs on the patio are perfect spots for a day spent lazing in the sun. If it gets too hot, cool rooms await indoors.

Shreyas Retreat's dining room serves delectable vegetarian cuisine with flavours from India, southern Europe and the Orient. Only the freshest herbs and vegetables, harvested from the property's own gardens, are used to prepare the sumptuous meals.

At Shreyas Retreat, the capable chefs are always willing to comply with special requests or specific dietary needs.

Guests are encouraged to be involved in the retreat's programmes, including its wellness classes and food cultivation. There are guided tours to its herb and vegetable gardens and rice fields, where guests learn about planting, weeding, watering and harvesting, all the steps necessary to ensure that what arrives at the dining table is nothing short of the finest.

Shreyas Retreat is very much inspired by the Indian spiritual practice of looking deep within the self in the search for answers to questions of existence and being. To deepen the sense of quietude and be more in tune with their inner selves, guests can attend daily yoga and meditation classes, or work with instructors on an individual basis. Lessons, which are non-denominational and suitable for everyone, cover various aspects of yoga and meditation including classical *Hatha* yoga, *Mouna* (silence), *Pranayama* (breathing techniques) and *Pratyahara* (internalising). A dedicated yoga hall provides ample space for these lessons, and the retreat's compound has many more areas specially created for quiet repose.

The central pool, which is heated and ozonated, is another way to recharge, as are the outdoor jacuzzi and indoor steam rooms.

Cricket holds a special place in the hearts of Indians, and if you have not tried the game before, the retreat runs net training sessions and has a professional bowling machine to assist those new to the sport.

A stay at Shreyas Retreat takes guests away from the stresses of life and puts them on the path towards rejuvenation. With its calm, natural surroundings, wholesome food, restorative spa therapies, and lessons in well-being, the retreat is truly a sanctuary for the world weary.

FACTS		
ROOMS	8 tents • 3 cottages • 1 three-bedroom cottage	
FOOD	vegetarian Indian, southern European and Oriental	
FEATURES	pool • spa • gym • cricket • library • walking track • yoga pavilion • amphitheatre • vegetable farm • herb garden	
BUSINESS	Internet access • conference hall • off-site facilitation	
NEARBY	traditional village • excursions to Belur, Bangalore, Mysore, Halebid and more	
CONTACT	Santoshima Farm, Gollahalli, Byrashetty Village, Nelamangala, Bangalore 562123, Karnataka • telephone: +91.80.2773 7103/7183 • facsimile: +91.80.2773 7016 • email: info@shreyasretreat.com • website: www.shreyasretreat.com	
OTHERS	no alcohol is allowed • smoking is restricted to certain areas	

Spice Coast Cruises

Kerala's vast backwaters provide a source of livelihood for many locals, and have done so for centuries. The best way to explore this complex system is on the water itself.

Spice Coast Cruises have one- and two-bedroom vessels styled after the traditional rice boat. Originally used only for work or as living quarters, these boats are now used for pleasure as well, to explore the backwaters.

The *kettuvallam* is the largest of the rice boats. With its spacious interior and regal carriage, it is a popular choice with

travellers. Every effort has been made to preserve the boat's authenticity and protect the environment it will be sailing through, so only natural materials are used in its construction. The hull uses the curved trunk of the jackfruit tree, while the interior features coir matting, split bamboo and palm fronds.

The vessels are also solar-powered and come fully equipped with a kitchen, bedroom with en suite bathroom, and living room. Most guests do not spend too much time in the bedroom, though, because the

THIS PAGE: *The boatman, who also acts as the navigator and cook, sets the vessel on its course through Kerala's historical backwaters.*

OPPOSITE: *The boat's living room is where guests spend most of their time, watching the world go by.*

best place to enjoy the breeze and stunning views is in the living room, while ensconced in a cosy rosewood-and-cane easy chair, or leaning back against the small bolsters at the front, enjoying the beautiful weather and the gentle splash of the water lapping against the sides of the private vessel.

Though by no means a slow boat—it travels at almost 10 km (6 miles) an hour, the cool breeze, salty air, clear sky and languid pace can be thoroughly sleep-inducing and utterly relaxing. But guests should not miss the many signs of bustling life beyond the banks: locals hard at work in the paddy fields, bodies bent almost double as their hands toil quickly in the shallow waters; children bathing at the water's edge, waving with delight at passing vessels; and other boats going along their way laden with rice, daily essentials and passengers. As the boat sails on, guests may catch the unmistakable scent of cinnamon, coconut and pepper from the surrounding spice plantations.

Meals onboard are kept simple but scrumptious, and are prepared by the boatman. And he prepares the best meal he knows how to—a meal fit for the gods, for traditionally, that is what guests are believed to be. Expect the evening's fare to begin with *kootu* or lentils and gourd, stirred with cracked pepper and mustard seeds, then garnished with roasted coconut shreds. The catch of the day is then served. It is typically marinated with red chilli, ginger and a dash of lime, before it is grilled to perfection. Fluffy white rice provides the staple.

All too soon, however, the day comes to an end with a blazing sunset, and it is time to retire to the comfortable confines of your bedroom, where the gentle rocking of the boat will lull you into a deep slumber.

FACTS		
ROOMS	2 one-bedroom boats • 2 two-bedroom boats
FOOD	Indian
FEATURES	solar-powered • en suite bathroom • living room • onboard navigator and cook
ITINERARY	cruise through the narrow canals of Alleppey and Kumarakom
CONTACT	Central Reservations, Casino Hotel, Willingdon Island, Cochin 682003, Kerala • telephone: +91.484.3011 711 • facsimile: +91.484.2668 001 • email: contact@cghearth.com • website: www.cghearth.com

PHOTOGRAPHS COURTESY OF SPICE COAST CRUISES.

Spice Village

Spice Village is a resort like no other. You will not find the usual sun, sand and sea combination here, and there are no major shopping centres or entertainment districts around for miles. In fact, Spice Village is a unique property set amidst centuries-old forests, rubber, coffee and spice plantations, and rolling highlands. It is located some 190 km (118 miles) from Cochin Airport, and the drive to the resort offers an apt introduction to this quiet property inspired by and built around nature.

The resort comprises a series of cottages designed to blend seamlessly into the surroundings. Each unit is built in the style of the original inhabitants of the land—the Mannans and Ooralies tribes, with brick, split bamboo and elephant grass, and distinctive grey thatch. Following the natural contours of the terrain, the cottages sit on varying gradients, leaving guests to follow gently meandering paths up or down to their respective residences.

Every cottage is simple in design and functional in form. The modern traveller may be shocked to find that there are no TVs in the cottages, but will soon come to understand that TVs are an unnecessary

THIS PAGE (FROM TOP): A shady path leads to the cottages; the scent of spices permanently perfumes the air around the pool and restaurant.

OPPOSITE: The cottages are reminiscent of the jungle abodes of the area's hill tribes.

accessory at Spice Village, especially when the surroundings provide so many more opportunities to engage the senses.

Spice Village lives up to its name in different ways. The air is always redolent with the smell of spices which the area is so well-known for, and which the resort carefully nurtures in its gardens. The cool, crisp air, lovely weather and relaxed pace of life provide for an idyllic getaway, hidden as the property is in the magnificent Periyar Hills. Holiday-makers love the resort for its air of romance, privacy and exoticism, while weary travellers treasure it as a sanctuary, a haven from the stresses of modern life.

The restaurant at Spice Village serves an international menu, though it should come as no surprise that the signature dishes are typically those which rely on the herbs and spices grown in the resort's own gardens. The chefs are generous with their timeless recipes, and often hold cooking demonstrations so that guests can not only

bring home wonderful memories of Spice Village, but also a wealth of culinary knowledge related to the region.

In the unlikely event that guests tire of strolling the gardens or exploring the myriad uses of herbs and spices, they can go

swimming or head out in a boat on Periyar Lake, trek through the forests, visit the nearby tiger reserve, or simply enjoy a game of badminton or tennis. Several indoor games are also available at the resort, should the weather disappoint.

FACTS		
	ROOMS	47 Standard Garden Cottages • 5 Deluxe Garden Cottages
	FOOD	international
	DRINK	Woodhouse Bar
	FEATURES	Ayurveda Centre • pool • cooking classes • badminton • tennis • indoor games
	BUSINESS	meeting room
	NEARBY	Periyar Wildlife Sanctuary • boat rides • trekking • spice plantation
	CONTACT	Central Reservations, Casino Building, Willingdon Island, Cochin 682003, Kerala • telephone: +91.484.3011 711 • facsimile: +91.484.2668 001 • email: contact@cghearth.com • website: www.cghearth.com

PHOTOGRAPHS COURTESY OF SPICE VILLAGE.

Surya Samudra Beach Garden

To stay at Surya Samudra Beach Garden is to experience another age. Spread over some 10 hectares (25 acres), this heritage property which comprises 21 villas looks as if it has been uprooted and transported to the present from a time long gone. The resort's staff will proudly tell you that your observations are correct—the villas were brought to this location from far-off villages, and re-constructed in an ancient style, albeit with modern conveniences.

Built on a rocky outcrop between two deserted beaches, every villa offers magnificent ocean views, along with an enclosed garden and verandah where guests can relax in total privacy. Wood is the dominant material used in the rooms, and is found on almost everything, from the polished floors to the walls, panelling, door and window frames, overhead beams and furniture. Antique sculptures and ornaments adorn each villa, while wall hangings showcase the local way of life. Because the villas offer all the comforts of home, many guests love to stay indoors, venturing out only for their meals.

THIS PAGE (FROM TOP): **The villas entice guests with vibrant colours and comfortable furnishings; ornate lamps, woven rugs and a liberal use of wood create a welcoming air.**

OPPOSITE (FROM LEFT): **The restaurant, Octopus, offers a choice of indoor and outdoor dining; the resort's unique pool was carved from a quarry.**

...looks as if it has been uprooted and transported to the present from a time long gone.

Like the villas, the resort's pool has its own story to tell. Constructed from an old quarry, it has a bare, rough-hewn floor. A specialist temple sculptor was engaged to turn the rock wall into a work of art, which he did beautifully. The infinity-edged pool's unique sculptures extend both above and below the surface of the water.

There are many ways to relax at Surya Samudra. From hammocks to garden furniture and poolside or beach loungers, guests are spoilt for choice when it comes to choosing the best seat in the house to enjoy a quiet morning or lazy afternoon. Whether strolling through the expansive compound, exploring the organic gardens, embarking on a sightseeing trip to nearby villages or going on a tour of Kerala's famous backwaters, the pace is as languid and relaxed as guests want it to be.

Neeramaya, the resort's Ayurveda and wellness spa, is renowned for its treatments. Whether for relaxation, rejuvenation or a specific ailment, the highly skilled therapists will be able to recommend something suitable from the extensive spa menu. Yoga and meditation go hand in hand with Ayurveda, and to meet this need, Surya Samudra has a yoga centre, with instructors available for group or private lessons.

FACTS		
	ROOMS	21 villas
	FOOD	Octopus: Mediterranean, Keralan and seafood
	DRINK	Bar-a-cuda
	FEATURES	pool • spa • yoga centre • reading lounge • boutique
	NEARBY	classical dances • martial arts • backwater cruises • temples • local villages
	CONTACT	Pulinkudi, Mullur PO Trivandrum 695521, Kerala • telephone: +91.471.2267 333 • facsimile: +91.471.2267 124 • email: info@suryasamudra.com • website: www.suryasamudra.com

PHOTOGRAPHS COURTESY OF SURYA SAMUDRA BEACH GARDEN.

Taj Malabar, Cochin

Many agree that Cochin is probably the best introduction to beautiful Kerala, and Taj Malabar, Cochin is one of the best starting points for any traveller embarking on an exploration of India's southwest.

Located on Willingdon Island, the hotel offers enviable views of Cochin Harbour, the picturesque Chinese fishing nets and the famous backwaters of Kerala.

Taj Malabar is the ideal place for visitors to fully experience the convergence of heritage and culture, history and tradition.

Built in the 1930s, the Heritage Wing of the hotel is predominantly composed of wood and brass, showcasing Kerala's expertise with these two materials. The guestrooms impress with a blend of old-world charm and contemporary appeal. They are designed to capture India's colonial history, with their teak flooring, woven sisal rugs, palm fronds and locally crafted wood artefacts and ornaments. All this is complemented by the most advanced amenities, including wireless Internet access and satellite TV channels.

Travellers used to the best in hotel accommodation rave about the Tower Wing's Executive Suite, with its breathtaking

THIS PAGE (CLOCKWISE FROM BELOW):
Guests have a host of dining options at their fingertips, including the casual and charming Rice Boat; the predominant use of wood lend the Deluxe and Executive suites an air of comfortable elegance.

OPPOSITE: The infinity-edged pool is where guests choose to relax by day. At night, private dining can be arranged here.

...a blend of old-world charm and contemporary appeal.

views, private balcony, traditional carved ceiling and four-poster bed. The Heritage Wing's Deluxe Suite, with polished interiors and a private garden, is a favourite with the hotel's business guests.

Island living takes on a whole new meaning at Taj Malabar. The design and décor of the aptly named Rice Boat, one of the hotel's restaurants, closely resembles a customary *kettuvalam* (rice boat), and the seafood menu pays tribute to the island location of the hotel. The restaurant's entrance is via a full-scale replica of a ship's bow while the interior sports a cane roof and swaying lanterns. Chefs at the open kitchen serve an array of seafood dishes originating from the historical stopovers of the rice barges.

All-day dining at Pepper is always a treat, with its array of Mediterranean, Italian, north Indian and Keralan options. When night falls, Dolphin's Point offers sumptuous barbecues and grills under a starlit sky, while Thai Pavilion serves authentic Thai cuisine.

A visit to Cochin would not be complete without a trip down Kerala's famous backwaters. These waterways meander past lush vegetation, rice fields and quaint villages, resulting in a long, serene and scenic cruise. To fully experience Kerala, opt for the cruise, and spice plantation and village visits, along with a trip to a traditional dance school organised by Taj Malabar.

FACTS

ROOMS	Heritage Wing: 25 Superior Rooms and 2 Deluxe Suites • Tower Wing: 49 Superior Rooms, 7 Deluxe Rooms and 7 Executive Suites
FOOD	Pepper: Mediterranean, Italian, north Indian and Keralan • Rice Boat: seafood • Thai Pavilion: Thai • Dolphin's Point: barbecues and seafood grills
DRINK	Tea Lounge • Mattancherry Lounge Bar • Aquarius Bar
FEATURES	Taamra Spa • *Cinnamon Coast* (a Taj luxury yacht) • pool • fitness centre
BUSINESS	Internet access • meeting rooms • business centre • secretarial services
NEARBY	backwater cruises • nature walks • golf • white-water rafting • spice plantations
CONTACT	Willingdon Island, Cochin 682009, Kerala • telephone: +91.484.266 6811/8010 • facsimile: +91.484.266 8297 • email: malabar.cochin@tajhotels.com • website: www.tajhotels.com

PHOTOGRAPHS COURTESY OF TAJ MALABAR, COCHIN.

The Taj West End, Bangalore

The lush gardens of The Taj West End, Bangalore are much welcomed by guests in search of respite from the frenetic pace of the city. The hotel is located a short distance from government offices and just 10 km (6.2 miles) from the city's main shopping, entertainment and business district, but guests may not even notice this as the hotel is nestled amidst some 8 hectares (20 acres) of beautiful greenery.

The Taj West End's accommodation options comprise a lovely mix of rooms and suites housed in mansions and villas. Every room overlooks the manicured grounds, offering views which epitomise the 'Garden City' Bangalore is renowned for being.

Each room is designed to provide the finest balance of form and functionality: spacious yet cosy, luxurious without being ostentatious, and contemporary in concept. Equipped with advanced technology such as wireless broadband Internet access, satellite TV, data ports and dual-line speaker phones, the rooms' amenities fully support the business needs of discerning travellers.

When it comes to club room facilities and services, The Taj Club Premium Rooms are in a class of their own. Aside from their classic and stylish décor, these rooms beat all the rest with their array of fine details including controlled lighting with dials within easy reach, silent air-conditioning units, marble or granite bathrooms, and plasma TV screens. They also come with a private verandah and courtyard—perfect for slowing the pace after a hectic day.

THIS PAGE (FROM TOP): The old-world charm of the hotel's architecture is complemented by its well-kept gardens; private verandahs allow natural light to filter into the rooms, making them even more inviting.
OPPOSITE: Get a taste of Vietnam in India at Blue Ginger.

A wonderful mix of dining choices is available at The Taj West End. Blue Ginger, which serves authentic Vietnamese food, has the honour of being the first Vietnamese restaurant in India. Its light, healthy and delicious fare has a loyal following.

India is well-known for its fiery curries and succulent seafood barbecues, and the Poolside Barbecue does both equally well. The Curry Wagon operates during lunch only, and when the sun sets, the fires start sizzling and the barbecue gets underway. Every evening, tantalising aromas fill the vicinity of the pool and draw guests with the promise of a sumptuous spread which always exceeds expectations.

Unlike most other city hotels, The Taj West End's Blue Bar is located in the garden. This casual but chic watering hole has an extensive menu of cocktails and wines, including an exciting range of Sangrias and other unique concoctions.

Being located in such a convenient spot allows the hotel to offer its guests many recreational options both within the hotel and in its vicinity; from workouts to swimming and tennis, and beyond its doors, horseback riding, golf, bowling, go-karting, paragliding and more. All this allows guests to make the most of their stay at The Taj West End.

FACTS		
ROOMS	27 Superior Rooms • 42 Luxury Rooms • 33 Club Rooms • 20 Suites	
FOOD	Mynt: Indian, Italian, Lebanese, Mediterranean • Blue Ginger: Vietnamese • Poolside Barbecue: curries and barbecues • pastry shop	
DRINK	Blue Bar	
FEATURES	fitness centre • pool • walking track	
BUSINESS	Internet access • meeting rooms • business centre • secretarial services	
NEARBY	Sammy's Dreamworld • FunWorld • bowling • fishing • go-karting • paragliding • rock climbing • trekking • golf • horseback riding • shopping	
CONTACT	Race Course Road, Bangalore 560001, Karnataka • telephone: +91.80.5660 5660 • facsimile: +91.80.5660 5700 • email: westend.bangalore@tajhotels.com • website: www.tajhotels.com	

PHOTOGRAPHS COURTESY OF THE TAJ WEST END, BANGALORE.

Trinity

Contemporary, chic and stylish, Trinity is the discerning traveller's choice for modern living. Located in the heritage centre of Fort Cochin, it is an exclusive boutique residence with only three suites—which explains its name. Everything about the property is fashionable, bright and bold, but despite its modern feel, the ambience is distinctly serene. Perhaps this effect is created by its compact size, or it could be the clean and uncluttered design, or even the generous spaces within each suite; but whatever the cause, Trinity is a favourite with those in search of a sanctuary.

Every suite is lavishly decorated with silk cushions, freshly pressed bedlinen, and convenient remote-controlled amenities. From air-conditioning to DVD and CD players and a well-stocked mini-bar, the interior is decidedly modern and upmarket, and more like a chic retreat than a hotel, thus adding to the intimate feel.

Each of the Red, Blue and Yellow suites has features that set them apart from each other. The Red Suite, the biggest of the three, is perfect for a family or small groups. Besides the comfortable king-size bed, there is an additional double-bed located in the suite's mezzanine, which is near enough for comfort, and far enough for privacy. The outdoor bathroom-cum-garden is always a hit with guests.

The Blue Suite, like the Red, also has a mezzanine, but here, guests will find an antique children's car, not a bed. This suite, too, has an outdoor bathroom within an enclosed garden. The Yellow Suite is adorned with outstanding black-and-white photographs of *kathakali* dancers. Unlike the usual dramatic pictures, however, these images show the dancers backstage, putting on their distinctive make-up. This suite comes with a spacious deck, making it a favourite with guests who love fresh air, natural light and unwinding outdoors.

Breakfast is usually served in the dining room. As there is no restaurant at Trinity, guests often make the 200-m (656-ft) walk across Fort Cochin's Parade Ground to the residence's sister property, Malabar House, for dinner. After a meal, unwind back at Trinity in the spacious living room, where guests can take their pick from bursting bookshelves or just play a game of cards.

THIS PAGE (FROM LEFT): Artworks by modern Indian artists are prominently displayed throughout the property; the mezzanine of the Red and Blue suites offers guests more space.
OPPOSITE: Each room is beautifully appointed, with lavish silk cushions and the generous use of dark wood.

FACTS		
	ROOMS	3 Luxury Suites
	FEATURES	Cinnamon Boutique • pool • Ayuverdic centre • butler service • bicycles
	BUSINESS	Internet access
	NEARBY	Jew Town • Mattancherry Place • St Francis Church • Vasco da Gama Church • Kishi Art Cafe • sightseeing tours • backwater cruises • Chinese fishing nets
	CONTACT	1/658 Ridsdale Road, Parade Ground, Fort Cochin, Kochi 682001, Kerala • telephone: +91.484.2216 669 • facsimile: +91.484.2217 777 • email: info@malabarhouse.com • website: www.malabarhouse.com

PHOTOGRAPHS COURTESY OF TRINITY.

Rajasthan Itinerary

There is no other place like Rajasthan, so colourful, so vibrant and utterly irresistible. A heavenly destination where an exotic past amalgamates perfectly with the present, Rajasthan offers the visitor enchanting cities, a dynamic culture and spellbinding wildlife.

For those interested in an action-packed itinerary, try safaris on camels, horses, elephants or jeeps at India's oldest hills, the Aravalis. For those more suited to a leisurely day outdoors, head out to the wetlands for a bit of bird watching to spot the many colourful feathered species in the area. And those inclined to indulge in a more relaxed and pampered stay can languish in the hospitality of Rajasthan's beautiful heritage properties.

Do not overlook Rajasthan's offerings for retail therapy at the many bazaars where visitors can pick up fantastic bargains that will keep them coming back for more.

THIS PAGE (CLOCKWISE FROM TOP): *Dine in comfort and opulence at The Oberoi, New Delhi; enjoy a luxurious night's sleep at Taj Lake Palace; wake up to a view of the Taj Mahal at The Oberoi Udaivilās.*

OPPOSITE (FROM TOP): *The regal façade of Rambagh Palace; guests at The Imperial, New Delhi's Heritage Rooms get a taste of a bygone era.*

A heavenly destination where an exotic past amalgamates perfectly with the present...

Highlights of the Region

Taj Mahal • Palace of Winds • Lake Pichola

Suggested Itinerary by Abercrombie & Kent Travel

- Fly to New Delhi with either British Airways or Virgin Atlantic Airlines.
- Transfer from the airport for a two-night stay at either The Imperial, New Delhi or The Oberoi, New Delhi.
- Transfer by private air-conditioned vehicle to Agra and stay for two nights at The Oberoi Amarvilās. Explore the wonders of the Taj Mahal.
- Drive to Jaipur via Fatehpur Sikri and stay at either Rambagh Place or The Oberoi Rajvilās for three nights.
- Fly from Jaipur to Udaipur for a three-night stay at either Taj Lake Palace or The Oberoi Udaivilās.
- Return flight via New Delhi.

Abercrombie & Kent Travel specialises in creating tailor-made holidays to India. With offices in Delhi, Agra and Jaipur, they are able to offer their clients the benefit of in-depth local knowledge and 24-hour support. This itinerary is fully flexible and merely offers an example of the type of programmes offered in Rajasthan, South India and the Himalayas. To discuss your holiday in this region, please call Abercrombie & Kent on +44.845 0700 615 or visit www.abercrombiekent.co.uk

South India Itinerary

Every district in Kerala has its own unique culture and characteristics. One aspect of the state's rich cultural heritage is manifested in its variety of religious architecture: ancient Hindu temples with copper-clad roofs, later Islamic mosques with 'Malabar gables', and colonial Portuguese Baroque churches. Splendid paintings, especially murals, exhibit distinct local traditions and styles. The land is also a flourishing centre of the *kathakali* dance form.

Kerala has been the playground for numerous travellers interested in its rich culture, exotic cuisine and romantic cruises along its many backwater canals. Visitors can also banish all tension with a relaxing traditional Ayurvedic massage which is based on a natural health science that has been passed down from generations.

Visit Kovalam, Kerala's most famous and picture-perfect beach ringed by groves of coconut trees and bask in the sun while in 'God's own country'.

Highlights of the Region

Kochi's exotic harbour • Kerala's tropical backwaters • Hindu beach temples

Suggested Itinerary by Abercrombie & Kent Travel

- Fly to Kochi direct with British Airways.
- Transfer from the airport for a two-night stay at either The Brunton Boatyard Hotel, Taj Malabar or Malabar House.
- Board The Oberoi, Motor Vessel Vrinda for a four-night backwaters discovery tour.
- Travel by road to Thekkady and stay overnight at Spice Village.
- Drive to Kumarakom and stay at the Coconut Lagoon.
- Onwards to Maraikulam for a two-night stay at Marari Beach Resort.
- Enjoy a morning drive back to Kochi for your onward flight.

Abercrombie & Kent Travel specialises in creating tailor-made holidays to India. With offices in Delhi, Agra and Jaipur, they are able to offer their clients the benefit of in-depth local knowledge and 24-hour support. This itinerary is fully flexible and merely offers an example of the type of programmes offered in Rajasthan, South India and the Himalayas. To discuss your holiday in this region, please call Abercrombie & Kent on +44.845 0700 615 or visit www.abercrombiekent.co.uk

THIS PAGE (FROM TOP): *The Victorian interior of the Superior Room at Taj Malabar's Heritage Wing; feel at home at Malabar House; enjoy the stunning backwaters of Kerala with Motor Vessel Vrinda.*

OPPOSITE (FROM TOP): *Tall coconut trees dot the grounds at Marari Beach Resort; poolside pleasures await at Coconut Lagoon.*

Himalayas Itinerary

Shimla has been blessed with all the natural bounties one can think of. Set in a panoramic location, this fascinating town is surrounded by green pastures and snow-capped peaks. The spectacular mountain location provides visitors with the perfect setting in which to unwind and experience some of India's finest and most relaxing Ayurvedic treatments.

Shimla was the summer capital of British India. Although colonial rule has long passed, its architectural heritage can still be experienced by visitors.

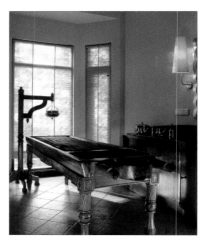

THIS PAGE (FROM TOP): *Feel tensions ease away with a traditional Ayurvedic massage at Ananda in the Himalayas; greet each day with a salutation to the sun at Wildflower Hall.*

OPPOSITE: *The Oberoi Cecil's classically elegant interiors with wood panelling give guests a glimpse of the days of the British Raj.*

Do not leave without strolling along the town's long stretch of purely pedestrian road for a shopping experience not found anywhere else in the world but at The Mall. Only select cars, ambulances and fire engines are allowed to intrude upon your personal time for retail therapy here.

Highlights of the Region

Ayurvedic spas • mountain peaks • stunning scenery

Suggested Itinerary by Abercrombie & Kent Travel

- Fly to New Delhi with either British Airways or Virgin Atlantic.
- Stay overnight at either The Imperial, New Delhi or The Oberoi, New Delhi.
- Transfer by train and car to reach either Ananda in the Himalayas, The Oberoi Cecil, Shimla or Wildflower Hall for a five-night stay.
- Return by train and car to New Delhi for an overnight stay prior to onward flights.

Abercrombie & Kent Travel specialises in creating tailor-made holidays to India. With offices in Delhi, Agra and Jaipur, they are able to offer their clients the benefit of in-depth local knowledge and 24-hour support. This itinerary is fully flexible and merely offers an example of the type of programmes offered in Rajasthan, South India and the Himalayas. To discuss your holiday in this region, please call Abercrombie & Kent on +44.845 0700 615 or visit www.abercrombiekent.co.uk

index

Numbers in *italics* denote pages where pictures appear. Numbers in **bold** denote map pages.

picturecredits

The publisher would like to thank the following for permission to reproduce their photographs:

Timothy Auger back cover: stairway, 65, 68, 69 (below), 74 (left), 101, 102 (top), 106, 107 (below)
John Brunton back cover: temple, 162, 166 (below), 168, 169 (top)
Corbis 12, 13, 14–15, 16 (top), 24, 26, 29, 30 (top), 31, 32, 34, 35, 36, 38, 39, 46, 51 (top), 52 (right), 55, 57, 64, 67, 70, 72 (top), 75 (below), 79 (below), 94, 103, 104, 107 (top), 133, 134 (right), 137 (below), 138 (top), 165 (centre), 172 (top), 174 (top), 176, 177
Devi Garh Fort Palace front cover: bed and table setting, 4, 5
Michael Freeman front cover: fire and wooden panel, back cover: floral design and jewellery, front flap: Taj Lake Palace, 19 (top), 20 (top), 21 (below), 23, 27 (top), 33 (below), 37, 48, 49, 50, 51 (below), 53, 54 (top and below), 66, 69 (top), 71 (top), 73, 74 (right), 77, 78, 80, 81, 96, 97, 98 (below), 100 (top and centre), 109, 128, 136–137, 163 (top)
Getty Images 62
The Imperial, New Delhi 72 (below)
Shari Kessler 28 (below), 30 (below), 56, 75 (top), 76, 98 (top), 102 (below), 163 (below)
The Leela, Goa front cover: candelabra, back cover: panel

Nitin Rai 17 (right), 100 (below), 140 (top), 164
The Oberoi Udaivilās, Udaipur back flap, back cover: pool, 2
The Park, Chennai 8–9
Rambagh Palace, Jaipur front cover: courtyard, 99
Reuters/alt.TYPE Images 52 (left), 165 (below), 178
Survey of India all maps
Taj Lake Palace, Udaipur front flap: bedroom and swing-seat
Luca Tettoni back cover: elephants and food, 15 (top), 16 (below), 17 (left), 8, 19 (below), 20 (below), 21 (top and centre), 22 (top), 54 (centre), 71 (below), 79 (top), 105, 108, 131, 132, 134 (left), 135, 138 (below), 139, 140 (below), 142, 143, 160, 165 (top), 166 (top), 167, 169 (below), 170, 171, 73, 174 (below), 175, 179
Tips Images front cover: textiles and hats, 28 (top), 130, 141, 172 (below)
Leisa Tyler 22 (below), 27 (below)
Wildflower Hall, Shimla in the Himalayas front cover: woman, 33 (top)

directory

Ahilya Fort
Maheshwar, Madhya Pradesh 451224
telephone : +91.11.5155 1575
facsimile : +91.11.5515 1055
info@ahilyafort.com
www.ahilyafort.com

Ananda in the Himalayas
The Palace Estate, Narendra Nagar,
District Tehri-Garhwal, Uttaranchal 249175
telephone : +91.13.7822 7500
facsimile : +91.13.7822 7550
sales@anandaspa.com
www.anandaspa.com

Bangaram Island Resort
Central Reservations, Casino Hotel,
Willingdon Island, Cochin 682003, Kerala
telephone : +91.484.3011 711
facsimile : +91.484.2668 001
bangaramisland@cghearth.com
www.cghearth.com

Bhandari Jewellers, Jaipur
5 Dashera Kothi, Amer Road,
Jaipur 302002, Rajasthan
telephone : +91.141.2630 654/
2630 658/2632 276
facsimile : +91.141.2630 632
vipulbhandari@hotmail.com
www.bhandarijewellers.com

The Brunton Boatyard Hotel
Central Reservations, Casino Hotel,
Willingdon Island, Cochin 682003, Kerala
telephone : +91.484.3011 711
facsimile : +91.484.2668 001
contact@cghearth.com
www.cghearth.com

Casino Hotel
Central Reservations, Casino Hotel,
Willingdon Island, Cochin 682003, Kerala
telephone : +91.484.3011 711
facsimile : +91.484.2668 001
contact@cghearth.com
www.cghearth.com

Coconut Lagoon
Central Reservations, Casino Hotel,
Willingdon Island, Cochin 682003, Kerala
telephone : +91.484.3011 711
facsimile : +91.484.2668 001
contact@cghearth.com
www.cghearth.com

Devi Garh Fort Palace
Village Delwara, Tehsil Nathdwara,
District Rajsamand,
Udaipur 313001, Rajasthan
telephone : +91.2953.289 211
facsimile : +91.2953.289 357
devigarh@deviresorts.com
www.deviresorts.com

Hotel de L'Orient
17 Rue Romain Rolland, Pondicherry 605001
telephone : +91.413.2343 067
facsimile : +91.413.2227 829
sales@neemranahotels.com
www.neemranahotels.com

The Imperial, New Delhi
Janpath, New Delhi 110001
telephone : +91.11.2334 1234
facsimile : +91.11.2334 2255
luxury@theimperialindia.com
www.theimperialindia.com

The Leela, Goa
Cavelossim, Mobor, Goa 403731
telephone : +91.83.2287 1234
facsimile : +91.83.1287 1352
leela@ghmhotels.com
www.theleela.com

The Leela Kempinski, Mumbai
Sahar, Mumbai 400059,
Maharashtra
telephone : +91.22.5691 1234
facsimile : +91.22.5691 1212
reservations@theleela.com
www.theleela.com

The Leela, Kovalam Beach
Trivandrum 695527, Kerala
telephone : +91.471.2480 101
facsimile : +91.471.2481 522
reservations.kovalam@theleela.com
www.theleela.com

The Leela Palace Kempinski, Bangalore
23 Airport Road,
Bangalore 560008, Karnataka
telephone : +91.80.2521 1234
facsimile : +91.80.2521 2222
reservations@theleelablr.com
www.theleela.com

Malabar House
1/268 + 1/269 Parade Road,
Fort Cochin, Cochin 682001, Kerala
telephone : +91.484.2216 666
facsimile : +91.484.2217 777
info@malabarhouse.com
www.malabarhouse.com

Marari Beach Resort
Central Reservations, Casino Hotel,
Willingdon Island, Cochin 682003,
Kerala
telephone : +91.484.3011 711
facsimile : +91.484.2668 001
contact@cghearth.com
www.cghearth.com

Neemrana Fort-Palace
Village Neemrana,
District Alwar 301705, Rajasthan
telephone : +91.494.246 006
facsimile : +91.494.246 005
sales@neemranahotels.com
www.neemranahotels.com

The Oberoi Amarvilās, Agra
Taj East Gate, Agra 282001,
Uttar Pradesh
telephone : +91.562.2231 515
facsimile : +91.562.2231 516
reservations@oberoi-amarvilas.com
www.oberoihotels.com

The Oberoi, Bangalore
39 Mahatma Gandhi Road,
Bangalore 560001, Karnataka
telephone : +91.80.2558 5858
facsimile : +91.80.2558 5960
reservations@oberoiblr.com
www.oberoihotels.com

The Oberoi Cecil, Shimla
Chaura Maidan, Shimla 171004,
Himachal Pradesh
telephone : +91.177.2804 848
facsimile : +91.177.2811 024
reservations@oberoi-cecil.com
www.oberoicecil.com

The Oberoi Grand, Kolkata
15 Jawaharlal Nehru Road,
Kolkata 700013, West Bengal
telephone : +91.33.2249 2323
facsimile : +91.33.2249 3229
reservations@oberoi-cal.com
www.oberoihotels.com

**The Oberoi, Motor Vessel Vrinda,
Backwaters of Kerala**
Corporate Marketing Division,
7 Sham Nath Marg, New Delhi 110054
telephone : +91.11.2389 0505
facsimile : +91.11.2389 0582
www.oberoihotels.com

The Oberoi, Mumbai
Nariman Point, Mumbai 400021, Maharashtra
telephone : +91.22.5632 5757
facsimile : +91.22.5632 4142
reservations@oberoi-mumbai.com
www.oberoihotels.com

The Oberoi, New Delhi
Dr. Zakir Hussain Marg,
New Delhi 110003
telephone : +91.11.2436 3030
facsimile : +91.11.2436 0484
reservations@oberoidel.com
www.oberoihotels.com

The Oberoi Rajvilās, Jaipur
Goner Road, Jaipur 303012, Rajasthan
telephone : +91.141.2680 101
facsimile : +91.141.2680 202
reservations@oberoi-rajvilas.com
www.oberoihotels.com

The Oberoi Udaivilās, Udaipur
Haridasji Ki Magri, Udaipur 313001,
Rajasthan
telephone : +91.294.2433 300
facsimile : +91.294.2433 200
reservations@oberoi-udaivilas.com
www.oberoihotels.com

The Oberoi Vanyavilās, Ranthambhore
Ranthambhore Road,
Sawai Madhopur 322001, Rajasthan
telephone : +91.746.2223 999
facsimile : +91.746.2223 988
reservations@oberoi-vanyavilas.com
www.oberoihotels.com

The Park, Bangalore
14/7 Mahatma Gandhi Road,
Bangalore 560042, Karnataka
telephone : +91.80.2559 4666
facsimile : +91.80.2559 4667
resv.blr@theparkhotels.com
www.theparkhotels.com

The Park, Chennai
601 Anna Salai,
Chennai 600006, Tamil Nadu
telephone : +91.44.5214 4000
facsimile : +91.44.5214 4100
resv.che@theparkhotels.com
www.theparkhotels.com

The Park, Kolkata
17 Park Street, Kolkata 700016,
West Bengal
telephone : +91.33.2249 9000
facsimile : +91.33.2249 4000
resv.cal@theparkhotels.com
www.theparkhotels.com

The Park, New Delhi
15 Parliament Street, New Delhi 110001
telephone : +91.11.2374 3000
facsimile : +91.11.2374 4000
tpnd@theparkhotels.com
www.theparkhotels.com

The Piramal Haveli at Bagar
Village and PO Bagar 333023,
District Jhunjhunu, Shekhavati, Rajasthan
telephone : +91.1592.221 220
sales@neemranahotels.com
www.neemranahotels.com

Rambagh Palace, Jaipur
Bhawani Singh Road,
Jaipur 302005, Rajasthan
telephone : +91.141.2211 919
facsimile : +91.141.2385 098
rambagh.jaipur@tajhotels.com
www.tajhotels.com

Serenity at Kanam Estate
Payikad, Kanam PO 686515 Vazhoor,
Kerala
telephone : +91.481.2456 353/
484.2216 666
facsimile : +91.481.2456 353
info@malabarhouse.com
www.malabarhouse.com

Shalimar Spice Garden Resort
Murikkady PO Kumily 685535,
District Idukki, Kerala
telephone : +91.4869.222 132
facsimile : +91.4869.223 022
shalimar_resort@vsnl.com
www.shalimarkerala.com

Shreyas Retreat
Santoshima Farm, Gollahalli, Byrashetty Village,
Nelamangala, Bangalore 562123, Karnataka
telephone : +91.80.2773 7103/7183
facsimile : +91.80.2773 7016
info@shreyasretreat.com
www.shreyasretreat.com

Spice Coast Cruises
Central Reservations, Casino Hotel,
Willingdon Island, Cochin 682003, Kerala
telephone : +91.484.3011 711
facsimile : +91.484.2668 001
contact@cghearth.com
www.cghearth.com

Spice Village
Central Reservations, Casino Building,
Willingdon Island, Cochin 682003, Kerala
telephone : +91.484.3011 711
facsimile : +91.484.2668 001
contact@cghearth.com
www.cghearth.com

Surya Samudra Beach Garden
Pulinkudi, Mullur PO
Trivandrum 695521, Kerala
telephone : +91.471.2267 333
facsimile : +91.471.2267 124
info@suryasamudra.com
www.suryasamudra.com

Taj Lake Palace, Udaipur
PO Box No. 5, Pichola Lake,
Udaipur 313001, Rajasthan
telephone : +91.294.2528 800
facsimile : +91.294.2528 700
lakepalace.udaipur@tajhotels.com
www.tajhotels.com

The Taj Mahal Palace + Tower, Mumbai
Apollo Bunder, Mumbai 400001, Maharashtra
telephone : +91.22.5665 3366
facsimile : +91.22.5665 0300
tmhbc.bom@tajhotels.com
www.tajhotels.com

Taj Malabar, Cochin
Willingdon Island, Cochin 682009, Kerala
telephone : +91.484.266 6811/8010
facsimile : +91.484.266 8297
malabar.cochin@tajhotels.com
www.tajhotels.com

The Taj West End, Bangalore
Race Course Road,
Bangalore 560001, Karnataka
telephone : +91.80.5660 5660
facsimile : +91.80.5660 5700
westend.bangalore@tajhotels.com
www.tajhotels.com

Trident Hilton Gurgaon
New Delhi National Capital Region,
443 Udyog Vihar, Phase V,
Gurgaon 122016, Haryana
telephone : +91.124.2450 505
facsimile : +91.124.2450 606
reservations.gurgaon@trident-hilton.com
www.gurgaon.hilton.com

Trinity
1/658 Ridsdale Road, Parade Ground,
Fort Cochin, Cochin 682001, Kerala
telephone : +91.484.2216 669
facsimile : +91.484.2217 777
info@malabarhouse.com
www.malabarhouse.com

The Verandah in the Forest, Matheran
Barr House, Matheran 410102,
District Raigarh, Maharashtra
telephone : +91.2148.230 296
facsimile : +91.2148.230 811
sales@neemranahotels.com
www.neemranahotels.com

Wildflower Hall, Shimla in the Himalayas
Chharabra, Shimla 171012,
Himachal Pradesh
telephone : +91.177.2648 585
facsimile : +91.177.2648 686
reservations@wildflowerhall.com
www.oberoihotels.com